Bali Raw

An exposé of the underbelly
of Bali, Indonesia

MALCOLM SCOTT

monsoon

monsoonbooks

First published in 2012
by Monsoon Books Ltd
www.monsoonbooks.co.uk

No.1 Duke of Windsor Suite, Burrough Court,
Burrough on the Hill, Leics. LE14 2QS, UK.

ISBN (paperback): 978-981-4358-71-2
ISBN (ebook): 978-981-4358-72-9

This 7th edition published in 2018

Cover design©Cover Kitchen

National Library Board, Singapore Cataloguing-in-Publication Data
Scott, Malcolm, 1966-
Bali raw / Malcolm Scott. – Singapore : Monsoon Books, 2012.
p. cm.
ISBN : 978-981-4358-71-2 (pbk.)
1. Bali Island (Indonesia) 2. Bali Island (Indonesia) – Social conditions.
3. Social problems – Indonesia – Bali Island. I. Title.
DS647.B2
959.86 -- dc22   OCN777441703

Printed and bound in Great Britain by Clays Ltd, Elcograf S.p.A.
20 19 18   7 8 9

Contents

I ams what I ams ... yuk, yuk, yuk
Popeye the Sailor

I am a good person but I do bad things sometimes
I am at best a good and bad person, aren't we all?
The author

Prologue

Since the early twentieth century and the Golden Age of Hollywood, Bali has been portrayed to the world as the paradise of paradises. But Bali is also violent, ugly and distasteful and living in Bali can be a game of survival.

This is the Bali that I know and that I have called home for almost a decade, a Bali where the fittest survive and those with the biggest wallet and the greatest connections endure.

There may be parts of this book where the reader will not like the author or his actions and there are certainly parts that I did not want to include. For better or worse I have decided not to sacrifice candour for likeability, I want this story to be honest and that means sharing actions that I'm not necessarily proud of.

This is the story of dog-eat-dog Bali, a palm-tree-laden prison where anything goes as long as you can afford it.

This is Bali Raw.

Surviving the Kuta Carnival

Bagus Bar, Kuta

"Would you like to live in Bali? This isn't a gift, you'll have to work and find yourself a role in the company. I'll pay you a hundred dollars a week for the first year, same as I paid myself. You can rent a room in Kuta and the company will pay for it."

"Yes."

"Don't answer so fast, this isn't a tropical holiday. Kuta is a shit hole, it's a fucking sewer. You can get whatever you want but it comes at a price, a price I'm not willing to pay if things go wrong. I have worked too hard to have you come here and fuck it up for me."

"Yes."

"I'm not joking; if you come here you will be expected to work. I will not accept drugs, I will not accept arguments and I will not accept you fucking up. You fuck up and it's over, you're my brother but one fuck up and I'll send you home. I couldn't give a shit."

"Yes."

"Time to take responsibility for yourself. I'm not bringing

you out here so I can look after you. I'm here to work and make a go of things. If that's what you want to come here for then OK, but if you want to come here and party, don't. I don't need it."

"Yes."

"I'll get the paperwork sorted. When you get home, go to the Indonesian Embassy and apply for a six-month working visa, I'll see you in a couple of weeks."

"Cheers, and thanks."

"Yeah, whatever, don't fuck up."

That's how the conversation went and I knew my brother meant exactly what he said. The company was going from strength to strength and I wasn't really needed. I had no skills to offer other than the fact that I was a brother and although that brought with it 100% loyalty and a level of trust that could not be found outside my family it was not a marketable skill elsewhere.

This may sound like an easy ticket but in my family being one of the brothers comes with its own responsibilities. During my life the respect of my counterparts was earned not gifted.

This applied to the four of us brothers; we all had to stand alone before we could stand as a group. People often ask why we are so close. For me this is the reason: my brothers and I grew up in a tough environment and we formed a mutual respect built on each other's solitary struggle. When you are living, working and partying in a place like Bali, being part of a family group like ours can be a very big asset.

I felt I had been given huge respect when I was offered a position in a company that three of my brothers had built over the last three years, but I knew I would have to earn my keep.

About two weeks before this meeting took place, I happened to be sitting in a bar in Bali when Billy, my younger brother, came storming in. I could see from Billy's face that something was wrong. His expression was uncharacteristically serious, and he had a ready-to-take-care-of-business look.

Billy didn't mess about. He walked up to my table and said, "Nick's in trouble, he's with the cunt that glassed him. The fuck is bringing his Bali boys down to get him."

No other words were exchanged, they didn't need to be. Billy walked out of the bar and hopped onto his motorbike and started the engine. I didn't bother to pay my bill; I followed and jumped on the back.

Billy gunned the engine and we took off through the back streets of Bali at a belting pace. This was serious. The person Billy was referring to had tried to murder my brother once before. Sitting on the back of that bike as we flashed through unfamiliar streets, I couldn't help but wonder if my older brother was already being bashed by a group of Balinese gangsters.

I have now lived in Bali for many years and the route we took that day is as familiar to me as the back of my hand, but at the time I didn't know where we were going. All I remember is agonising that we would somehow become lost and not make it in time to help Nick.

To this day I don't know how we did make it. Billy drove like a maniac. The motorbike screamed in agony as we shot past cars, through alleyways and in front of trucks. More than once we came perilously close to having an accident.

I was incredibly relieved when Billy finally pulled up at a set of traffic lights and pointed to a restaurant across the road. "He's in there!" he shouted. I knew Billy would have to get the bike through the lights and across the road but I didn't need to be told twice. I leapt off the back, kicked off my thongs and sprinted through the oncoming traffic towards the restaurant.

I had no doubt Billy would follow as soon as he was able; he is one of the staunchest men I have ever met and there would be no stopping him once he could dump the bike. When I reached the restaurant door I yanked it open and charged inside. Nick was seated at a table and across from him sat a guy with a ponytail. "Motherfucker," I screamed and rushed him.

* * *

Eleven years ago, Nick and Billy started a successful business from scratch in Bali, an environment that is definitely not business friendly. After four years Nick took over the reins of the business and in the ensuing years he has had more things thrown at him than I believe any man or businessman should have to endure. But my brother Nick is a hard man; he never takes a backward step in life, in business or in a confrontation. Bali has done its best to tame Nick and it has failed. Somehow Nick has managed to knock down any obstacle that has been put in his way. Being stabbed in the throat with a broken Bintang beer bottle was one of those obstacles.

There is a syndrome of Western men wanting to save

Indonesian working girls that afflicts far too many expats in Bali. A bloke will go out with an Indonesian prostitute for a while, tell her to get off the game, give her a bundle of cash so she can afford to stop working and then he will convince himself that she is being faithful. This works sometimes, but in my experience it happens rarely. Too often, the guy chooses the wrong kind of girl—the fact she is on the game to begin with should raise red flags—and he is surprised when the girl ends up back on the game as soon as his back is turned. The bloke that stabbed my brother in the neck happened to be dating an ex-working girl who was playing around and he settled on Nick as the guy she had cheated with. I will call this person Ankle as it sounds like his real name, and being lower than an arsehole it suits him.

Nick tells me he didn't have sex with Ankle's girlfriend, and I have no reason not to believe him, but he's also said to me, "Even if I did fuck her what would it matter? The girl was a hooker, she probably fucked a thousand blokes before Ankle and she probably fucked a thousand blokes after him." Having lived in Bali for as long as I now have, I would certainly back this statement.

Supposedly, Ankle was a gun runner out of Melbourne or Sydney and he considered himself well connected in Australia and in Bali. He had lived in Bali for some time so this was quite possible but it is wise to take any statement an expat makes about himself with a pinch of salt.

Although I never saw Ankle standing and I would only meet him the one time, I would guess that he was about thirty-five and five ten in height. His build was slim but muscular. The main thing that stood out to me about Ankle was his long ponytail;

I would notice this because I used it against him in our one and only encounter.

One evening at Bounty nightclub, Ankle came up to Nick and accused him of sleeping with his prostitute girlfriend. Nick told Ankle in no short terms that he hadn't slept with the girl and that Ankle should fuck off and find someone else to accuse. But Ankle wasn't interested.

Every time Nick turned around, Ankle was in his face. I know my brother well enough to understand that this is not a good idea. Nick has a quick temper and he doesn't suffer fools gladly. Apparently Ankle came up to Nick three times before Nick decided he'd had enough.

Nick asked Ankle to step outside the nightclub and they went down to Legian Street to sort out the problem. I will not go into the full details of the fight—I wasn't present and fights are at best blurry occasions that most people have a hard time remembering, also the following events take precedent over fisticuffs in the street. Suffice to say, the fight between Nick and Ankle ended with Ankle being knocked down on the road and Nick deciding he had had enough and walking away.

This is something Nick would later regret, as he tells it he had a chance to finish Ankle off but he took pity on the guy.

"The guy was in love with a prostitute and I had just put him on his arse in front of her, how could I not feel sorry for him?"

Ankle must have been deeply in love with this hooker because despite being let off with a few punches in a fair fight, he just wouldn't let it drop.

When the crowd had dispersed and Nick had left the scene

Ankle picked up a Bintang beer bottle, and, smashing it to make a dangerous weapon, he followed Nick down the street. When Nick turned into an alley to make his way home, Ankle confronted him.

Nick wanted none of it. To his mind he had beaten Ankle in a fair fight and he had let him off a more severe beating, by now he had walked a distance and he intended to get home and sleep off the incident. Nick didn't realise Ankle was carrying a smashed bottle but he turned to face him in case he decided to attack.

Ankle mouthed abuse and when he got too close for comfort Nick asked Ankle if he wanted to go another round. Nick didn't want to fight but he could not see a way out of the situation; he'd put Ankle down once and he had no doubt he could do it again.

Even armed, Ankle was afraid to confront Nick face to face. Ankle backed off and apologised. He then walked past Nick, keeping the broken bottle hidden at his side. Nick decided to let sleeping dogs lie; he walked off in another direction and entered another back lane that would take him to his hotel.

Ankle attacked Nick from behind like a true coward. Nick didn't hear him coming and was taken completely off guard. Ankle thrust the broken bottle into my brother's neck when he wasn't looking, he then ran away leaving my brother to die, abandoned in a Bali alley.

Nick felt a mighty blow then fell to his knees. He watched as Ankle ran down the alley away from him. Nick reached up to his neck and found the wound, hot blood gushed down his arm, down his shirt and into the street. His hand slipped into the massive hole the broken bottle had left in his neck. He felt himself passing out and he thought he would die. He slumped against a wall unsure what had happened, then clutched at his neck and looked down at the ground. At his side he saw the broken Bintang bottle resting in a pool of his own blood.

Nick told me that he thought it was all over but then suddenly an image of his children back in Australia came to him; he said he could imagine their devastation at hearing their father had died in an alley in Bali.

That single thought pressed him into action.

He forced himself to stand. He didn't want to die, he wanted to make it back to the main street, he wanted to at least try and get himself help, but most of all Nick wanted to see his children again. He found his feet and using a wall to keep himself upright he managed to claw his way back to the lights of Legian Street. Doctors would later tell him that he should have died after the initial blow—his artery had been slashed and he would have endured massive shock. They said it was a miracle that he had survived let alone managed to do all he did after the attack.

Nick has told me that death wasn't an option, if only for his children he wasn't going to allow that to happen. Somehow he made it to Legian Street, and as luck would have it a taxi pulled up and offered him a ride. He ripped open the door and thrust himself inside, screaming at the driver to take him to a hospital.

The taxi driver saw the blood flooding from Nick's neck wound and began to protest; he didn't want Nick's blood all over his car and he demanded Nick get out of the taxi. Nick screamed blue murder at the driver and he refused to get out. Nick then reached into his pocket and yanked out his wallet, there happened to be a bundle of cash inside, money for a building project.

Nick threw the cash at the driver. "Get me to a hospital now!" he demanded.

The driver grabbed the cash, gave it a quick count, then relented; he put his foot down and made his way to the nearest international hospital. The journey would normally take about fifteen minutes but due to the lateness of the hour and the taxi driver's distress it probably took around ten.

Nick lay back on the taxi seat, he knew he was in a very bad way. He was losing a lot of blood and he could possibly die, there was no one to help Nick but himself, he knew he had to stop the bleeding. He used the image of his children to keep himself going and with all the strength he could muster he reached for the wound and thrust his fingers into the gaping hole in his neck.

Nick fumbled around and tried desperately not to pass out. Eventually he found what he believed to be the severed artery. He groped for both sides then clamped down tight on the severed ends, doing his best to stem the bleeding. Then he laid back and tried to relax so that he didn't bleed out.

He told me that he lost grip of his artery many times on the journey, each time he would go through the same process of frantically clamping the vessels shut while trying not to pass out.

This took monumental courage, strength and will on his part and although he rarely talks about it, when it does come up, Nick always reiterates that it was the thought of his children losing their father and the effect it would have on them that pulled him through and kept him conscious despite the pain.

Nick finally made it to the hospital only to be refused

admission; the staff told Nick that his injuries were too severe and they did not have the equipment or expertise to operate.

The hospital staff did however use their ambulance to rush Nick to Sanglah Public Hospital in Denpasar.

When they arrived at Sanglah Hospital Nick was immediately wheeled into the Emergency Department where he underwent surgery. The doctors and nurses at Sanglah did an amazing job; Australian doctors would later look at the surgery they had performed and marvel at their professionalism and ability despite their rudimentary equipment. They told him that he was a very lucky man to have had such people working on him.

Nick had to endure numerous surgeries, he lost half his body weight and he now carries a twelve-inch jagged triangular scar running across the side of his throat and lower jaw line. He lived but it was a close call. He spent four weeks in an Indonesian hospital before he could fly home to Australia.

Ankle on the other hand ran like a cockroach. He packed up his things and disappeared the following day. That was until about a year later when Nick had a chance encounter with him in an upmarket Bali restaurant. Nick and his wife had gone there to buy bread and, as they turned to leave, Nick saw Ankle trying to sneak out a back door. Nick grabbed him by his ponytail and forced him into a chair. "You owe me big time, motherfucker," he said. Nick would not allow Ankle to leave and he told him as much; they could sort out the situation then and there by financial means or Nick would take Ankle into the carpark and injure him to the same level that he himself had been injured. Ankle did not know that Nick had already sent his wife to pay off the restaurant security staff.

Nick's wife is as tough and staunch a person as you are likely to meet. Ankle would not have been able to leave even if he'd tried but if he had managed to get past Nick and the security, I have no doubt that Nick's wife would have tackled him to the ground.

Nick has never gone into the full details of this first contact and I don't blame him. Ankle had nearly killed him and it must have taken huge restraint not to attack and try to inflict a similar injury.

This initial meeting went on for about ten minutes and while they spoke Nick noticed that Ankle was frantically sending out text messages. When he inquired about this, Ankle boasted that he had been in touch with his boys: Indonesian gangsters that doubled as security. He said they would be down at the restaurant to get Nick within ten minutes. Nick could have destroyed Ankle and made good his escape but that isn't his style. He made a phone call of his own and five minutes later Billy entered the pub where I was drinking and we both jumped on his motorbike.

* * *

When I leapt from the back of the motorbike and started running toward the restaurant where Nick and Ankle were I was pretty wound up. The dangerous ride through Bali streets, the rage for what had happened to my brother and the stress of what could be happening had all combined into a torrent of adrenalin and anger.

I didn't know what to expect when I charged through the doors. Clever, as always, Nick sat facing the front door. Seated across from him and with his back to me was Ankle. I glanced at Nick and was glad to see he was OK—at least he wasn't dealing with a load of gangsters. Oblivious to the fact that I was in an expensive restaurant, I screamed "motherfucker" and rushed towards the guy with the ponytail. Nick stood up and stopped me in my tracks. "Settle down Mal," he said, "we're sorting things out business style."

I slowed down because Nick had asked me to, but I still walked towards Ankle. I wanted a good look at the guy who had done so much damage. I stepped up to his side and stared down at him.

Ankle turned to look at me and gave me an aggressive stare. "What the fuck do you want?" he asked.

I smiled. "Yeah, you fuck. Is that what you think, is it?" I replied and grabbed Ankle by the ponytail. I yanked his head back hard. "How about I stab you in the fucking neck?"

He struggled but did not get up. Whimpering, he grabbed hold of the table and tried to pull his head away. I guess he didn't think I would come on with such ferocity.

Nick flew around from his side of the table, grabbed me by the arm and pulled me backwards. I kept hold of Ankle's hair and nearly yanked him from his seat. Nick spun around and got in front of me; he put his hands on my chest and looked into my eyes. "Stop it Mal, let him go; we are going to sort this out in a business fashion."

I gave Ankle's ponytail a final pull, and then dropped it. I moved around so I faced him, then bent forward. "You're dead," I hissed.

Nick forced his body between Ankle and me, gave me a shove and pushed me back a few steps. "Enough, I'm getting it sorted."

I wanted nothing more than to hit the bastard that had stabbed my brother in the throat. Nick is probably the only person that could have stopped me. Despite how much hatred I had for the guy it was Nick's deal and his call.

Nick held up his hand, "Mal, I'm going to sit down and Ankle and me are going to make a business deal." Nick caught my eye and shook his head slightly, "No more. Not yet anyway."

I took the hint. I watched Nick closely and could tell he was secretly pleased, it seemed a little bit of threat could help further the deal. I edged around and moved a little closer to Ankle; I now stood at his side. Ankle looked up at me nervously and I smiled what I hoped was an intimidating smile. "OK, Nick," I said, "I won't do anything. Not yet, anyway!" I wanted Ankle to realise his reprieve had a time limit.

Nick and Ankle went back to talking and then Billy suddenly charged through the door of the restaurant, took a look around and without hesitation rushed towards Ankle.

Billy is a bulldozer of a man and a hitting machine; once he starts he is almost impossible to stop. Nick knew he had to react quickly. He leapt from his chair once again and blocked him. "Billy stop!" he screamed into his face.

Billy tried to push past but Nick grabbed him bodily, the two of them wrestled. Nick only just managed to hold Billy back. Billy settled and Nick walked him backwards. "Billy slow down, leave it," he said, "this is now business, it's about money."

Billy looked passed Nick and stared at Ankle. "Yeah, you

know who I am," he said over Nick's shoulder. "You want to hurt my family, come and try me, motherfucker!"

Nick stood face to face with Billy; he spoke calmly and tried to pacify him. I took the opportunity to step behind Ankle and again grabbed him by the hair then shoved his face forward. Ankle struggled but I held him firmly by his ponytail. I put my mouth close to his ear, "You like to stab people from behind, how about I rip this off?" I gave the ponytail a yank. "What do you think of that?" I asked.

Ankle tried to stand but I held him tightly, I could have punched him and I would have liked too. I relented and shoved his head forward. Then I let him go and stepped back.

Billy calmed down and Nick put an arm about his shoulder. "No fighting, Billy, I want this to be a business deal," he said, then led him over to the table. Billy walked around the table and stood on the other side of Ankle; we both stared down at the guy that had nearly killed our brother.

Nick stood across from Ankle. The emotion in the restaurant was high and close to explosion. We surrounded Ankle and a fight could have started at any moment. The only thing holding Billy and me back was the respect we held for Nick. If Billy had struck Ankle I would have been right behind him. Ankle had attacked my brother from behind with a broken bottle and I hated him for what he'd put Nick through. I would have had no qualms about joining the fight.

Nick is the oldest brother and incredibly protective, there was no way he would let his two younger brothers fight for him. If Billy had sparked off, Ankle would have had all three of us to contend with. Ankle knew it and he started shivering. The only one protecting him was the guy he had stabbed in the throat, he was right to be afraid.

Nick continued to hold Billy and me back from Ankle with words; he looked at us as though we were bad children then raised a finger and said. "Enough you two, I've got it sorted. Thank you, but let me deal with this."

Nick sat down at the table. "So, are your boys coming?" he asked.

Ankle stared at Nick and he tried to play the tough guy. He clenched his motorcycle keys in his fist, a metal key sticking out from between his knuckles. "They'll come."

I bent down close to him. "I hope you get a chance to use that," I whispered.

Billy inched closer, he didn't say anything but his presence reeked of danger; he put a hand down on the table to let Ankle know he was there. Ankle flinched and turned to glance at Billy.

I laughed loudly and Ankle turned back to me. He didn't know where to look. He made to stand but Billy placed a hand on his shoulder and shoved him back into the chair.

Nick smiled and gestured towards the key in Ankle's fist. "Well, it's been a long time." He looked at his watch, "Maybe they aren't going to make it. If I was you I would think about that before I tried to be a hero." Ankle slumped forward, slid the key back into his hand and didn't answer.

Nick smiled a chilling smile. "My boys are here and my Indonesian crew will be here at any moment. I have a feeling no one is coming for you."

Ankle sat motionless and fingered his key. "What is this, the fucking mafia?" he croaked.

Nick laughed, "Go ahead, make another call, get your protection down here." He reached over and gently pushed Ankle's phone towards him. Ankle looked at his phone but didn't pick it up.

"Fuck this," he said, and Billy and I crowded in.

Nick took the initiative and stopped us from going further. "Ankle's going to pay five thousand dollars; it's for my medical expenses." He spoke to Billy and me but delivered the message to Ankle.

Ankle looked around, he looked panicked, beaten. "OK," he blurted, "I'll pay, but I need time to get it together. Who will collect it?"

Nick leaned back in his chair; Billy and I edged back to give Ankle room. "I will send our security. A guy called Rap will come and collect over the next three months. Are you OK with that?" Rap was our Balinese security guard at the time, he was a scary-looking dude with a bat tattooed across his forehead. I wouldn't have liked him to turn up at my door demanding money.

Ankle agreed to the deal, Nick and he exchanged phone numbers and Nick collected his address. "Rap will come to your house tomorrow for the first payment."

Nick got up to leave and he beckoned Billy and me to follow. "OK, we'll leave it at that. You can fix up my bill," he smiled at Ankle. "Think of it as a down payment."

Billy gave Ankle a pat on the shoulder and the three of us brothers walked out together.

This may seem like extortion, and it probably was to a degree, but Ankle got off lightly. Nick's medical bills came to a lot more than five thousand dollars, not to mention the damages he would have been able to seek if the incident had occurred in a Western country. To my mind Ankle also deserved to be in jail for attempted murder.

I can't speak for Billy but as far as I was concerned it wasn't about the money, I acted on emotion. I hated Ankle for what he had done and would have gladly seen him hurt; at the very least I hoped I scared him.

Once outside I couldn't resist a final parting shot. I let Nick and Billy get in front and then I turned and walked back inside. For the first time I noticed a bunch of well-dressed patrons sitting around the restaurant. Visibly shaken, they just stared at me.

Ankle sat at the table traumatized. I walked up to him and leaned in close. Ankle flinched away from me. "Don't pay," I whispered, "I want this to be the last face you ever see." I smiled and turned to leave, and as I did I saw Billy enter from another door. I'm sure Billy went up and spoke to Ankle after I'd gone. I don't know what he said, he has never told me, but I know it wouldn't have been nice.

Nick, Billy and I went to a pub. Nick thanked us and we had a beer and a laugh. I'm sure Ankle wasn't laughing that night.

Ankle paid two thousand dollars towards Nick's medical bill then disappeared from Bali and hasn't been seen since.

Turn the Other Cheek

Bali is a rough place. You don't see it in the brochures, and the Indonesian press is very careful about what it prints, but the truth is there is always something going down. Tourists get robbed, raped and murdered and Westerners get in fights amongst themselves and with Indonesians on a regular basis.

Indonesians fight and kill each other all the time. There is huge animosity between different Balinese villages, between different Indonesian ethnic groups, and of course between Indonesians and Westerners. Balinese gangs control the security in most of the night spots and they hurt or kill each other in turf wars. Tourists often get bashed at nightclubs either by other punters or by the security. Expats fight each other. If you want to live in Bali, you better believe it is the Wild, Wild West and as dangerous a place as you will ever encounter.

About a month after I arrived in Bali to live I was attacked while walking through a nightclub. Someone decided to take me out and they did it with a king hit. This was not Ankle related, it was a random attack.

I had spent the night chatting to a Japanese computer expert who I thought could help me with my new role in the company. I had been given control of the company website and I thought the

Japanese guy could give me some advice. I spent the later part of the evening talking to a big South African guy, who had happened to grow up in the same place as a friend of mine. All innocent stuff.

I had just excused myself from the South African and was making my way to the toilet when I found my path blocked. I asked some guy if he could move his chair so that I could get past and I even said "excuse me". The next thing I knew, a huge tattooed arm come out of nowhere and slammed into the side of my face. I was sent sprawling through the crowd and ended up in the middle of the dance floor. I tried to stand and defend myself but my legs were jelly; I slipped back to the floor and flopped around in my blood like a landed fish. I was semi-conscious with people staring at me and half my face was caved in. I had a broken nose and a crushed cheekbone, and no one bothered to lend a hand.

Then I saw the Indonesian security heading my way and I knew I was in trouble. These guys didn't mess about and I was an easy target. Again I tried to stand but I could only just make it to my knees. The crowd parted to let the security through and I was grabbed roughly by the back of my shirt. Luckily, the huge South African I had been talking to earlier stepped between me and the security; he pushed them away, then hoisted me to my feet and put a protective arm about my shoulder.

The South African was a big guy, about six two and a hundred and ten kilos—he was a formidable-looking character and I was very glad he'd come to my rescue. The security was adamant that they wanted me for causing trouble but the South African faced them down. I was in no shape to protect myself or argue my point but he would not let them near me.

The security and the South African argued back and forth while I dripped blood onto the floor. I listened but I was fighting hard not to black out.

Eventually the security relented and they told the South African to take me outside; they said they didn't want me in their club. I was pretty sure I didn't want to be in their club either.

The big South African put an arm about my waist and carried me outside—he ended up covered in my blood and for that I was sorry. It was a big sacrifice for him to make when he was on holiday and just wanted to have fun.

My South African saviour did his best to straighten my broken nose, and then he sent me stumbling down the street to get away as fast as possible. I remember thinking as I staggered down the road with my face caved in, welcome to Bali. When I got home, I didn't go to hospital but called my brother Billy and his Indonesian wife; they came and picked me up and nursed me back to health.

I felt I had hit rock bottom that night, I didn't want to call my brother for help but I had no choice. I felt isolated in a foreign land that I didn't understand. I wondered why the security hadn't gone after the guy who king hit me. Now I know better. I was incredibly lucky that night; I now know from experience that I would have received a kicking from the Indonesian security guards if they had dragged me outside. Indonesian security go after the weak, not the strong. I was an easy target—a Westerner they could hurt without repercussion. After many years in Indonesia, and a lot of time spent in Bali nightclubs, I have seen this scenario play out dozens of times, and inevitably it is the person that is down that gets the beating.

That night I missed Australia and I didn't want to live in Bali anymore. I didn't want to live in a place where people stabbed you with bottles or bashed you when you were minding your own business. In the end it turned out to be a great lesson, but at the time I knew I had to toughen up if I was going to survive living in Indonesia.

I spent the next two weeks lying on my brother's couch recovering and letting my face heal sufficiently so I could return to work. And by the time I recovered I had found out who had punched me—evidently it was just a random act of violence by a Hawaiian surfer.

Our own Indonesian security offered to have him bashed. They assured me that the guy who had punched me would be set upon by five or six heavy Indonesians; they promised me he would not walk back onto his plane. I declined this offer as I didn't want to bring disrepute to my brother's business, but truth be told I did go through the motions. One night I sat outside the guy's hotel with the security to identify him, but in the end I put a hold on the bashing.

In the end I decided to let bygones be bygones and the guy who took a pot-shot at me got off lightly. Had I been a different person, the Hawaiian surfer may have found himself in deep trouble. It is always wise to know who you are dealing with in a place like Indonesia.

When the Bell Tolls

When I first came to live in Bali my employment package consisted of one hundred dollars per week and a one-bedroom apartment. This was to be reviewed after one year and I think for the second year I ended up with one hundred and fifty per week, so even for Bali things were pretty tight.

The apartment I moved into was tiny, basically a hotel room with a small stove. When I walk into it nowadays I can't believe I managed to live there for two years. I used to think of it as a prison and believe me it's not that different. There are so many metal bars on the windows, doors and across the front balcony that the place could be mistaken as a holding cell for the criminally insane and I believe if I had lived there any longer than I did I may have ended up as just that.

The apartment is situated in the very dark heart of Kuta, in one of the seedier parts of town. Across the road, no more than fifteen steps away, was a pub and next door to that a CD shop. Most nights the pub would crank up the music until about 1 am, then every morning at 7 am the young girl in the CD shop would play Bryan Adams at full volume. I didn't get much sleep and I came to loath Bryan Adams.

The only thing that kept me from losing it was the fact that the young girl was extremely pretty. Once in a while I would pull myself out of bed and get ready to march across the road and explode and then I would see her and fold enough to crawl back into bed humming a Bryan Adams tune—it's amazing the soothing effect a pretty face can have on a man.

Something you notice about Indonesians when you live amongst them is they like noise and they are extremely competitive. One of the problems I had with the CD shop and the pub was they would engage in musical duels every morning—the guy who opened the pub was a Guns N' Roses fan.

The girl would get there first and put on her Bryan Adams, then "Sweet Child of Mine" would come on and drown her music out so she would turn her music up and he in turn would crank up his sounds. It was bizarre, they both had good stereos and they would both play them at full volume every morning. I'm sure neither one could hear a thing or make out their songs. I, on the other hand, would lie in bed screaming my head off for them to shut the fuck up while my windows vibrated around me.

This went on for two years but I never walked outside and complained, there would have been no point. The Indonesians in Kuta live day to day—any complaint I made would last for that day, the next morning the same thing would have happened.

Another source of noise pollution I endured at that apartment was from a dog I nicknamed Tinkerbelle. Tinkerbelle was a little white fluffy dog that had an enormous bell tied about its neck; the bell would not have been out of place in a cathedral.

Tinkerbelle's owners must have decided it would be a good thing to let their dog stroll about the streets of Kuta at 3 am every morning and Tinkerbelle, God bless her, decided that my street and specifically the front of my apartment was the perfect place to hang out.

I must have complained about Tinkerbelle a lot in those days and one night, during a drinking session with my brother Billy and his wife, Tinkerbelle happened to stroll past with her huge bell. Ever protective, my brother's Indonesian wife turned to me and asked, "Is that Tinkerbelle?"

Thinking little of the question I replied that it was and went back to my conversation. I failed to notice my brother's wife pick up the air rifle that I had in my room, or the handful of bullets, and step outside. What I did notice, however, was Tinkerbelle's yelps of pain and the little white dog's bell ringing frantically.

"What the fuck?" I said to Billy, and we raced outside to see what was going on.

We saw Billy's wife chase the little dog down the street. She stopped and raised the rifle to her shoulder, fired a couple of shots into the poor dog, then followed in hot pursuit. Poor Tinkerbelle took two shots in the side, she yelped then dodged left and right. Billy's wife stopped, took aim and fired again—she scored another direct hit.

Tinkerbelle finally escaped and Billy's wife marched back to where we stood with the air rifle over her shoulder. "I shot that Tinkerbelle," she said with an air of pride.

"Thank you," I said, slightly bewildered by what I had witnessed. I hated the dog but I didn't want to kill it. "You really didn't have to do that."

My brother's wife walked back inside, placed the rifle down

as though she had just returned from an African safari and announced: "That fucking Tinkerbelle was disturbing my brother, so I shot it."

I'm not sure if my brother's wife killed Tinkerbelle but the little dog never disturbed me again.

I also learned a valuable lesson: do not get an Indonesian woman angry. Cute and fluffy or not, they will shoot you.

Losing Helmets

In Bali there is a grey area between prostitution and girls who want a fun time and sometimes ask for money. Not all the Indonesian girls who party at nightclubs are prostitutes, despite the fact that they will sometimes ask for money, drinks or to be taken shopping. An Indonesian girl who cannot afford the entry fee or who doesn't have monery for drinks or clothes may ask for money or some form of payment if she thinks a man wants to date her or sleep with her. She will see this as a normal and if the man refuses she will see him as tight.

She may not see this as full prostitution; after all, she wants what any Western girl takes for granted: to be able to go out with her friends, dance and have fun, and eventually to meet someone she can form a relationship with. This took me a long time to learn and for most Western men it is a hard concept to grasp, but as with most forms of generalisation the reality rests with the individual.

Traditionally, Indonesian women are taught that it is the woman's role to look after the man when it comes to home life and it's the man's role to look after the woman financially. Indonesian girls are paid very little money and they are expected to work very long hours; six days a week and twelve-hour shifts are the norm and many a young Indonesian girl has rotted her life away slogging it out for one hundred Australian dollars a month in a mini mart. She can't afford to go out and she is too tired to go out. All Indonesian girls are expected to send at least part of the money they earn back to their family, what is so bad about the man she is willing to give her body to, if not her heart, helping out a bit, especially if he is a rich Westerner?

Naturally there are also many Indonesian women who will not sleep with a man unless there is some kind of attraction, even if the man is willing to pay a lot of money. Western women take into account a man's prospects, so do Indonesian women; make no mistake there are Indonesian girls who are picky when it comes to Westerners they date and/or sleep with. They may not ask for money up front but a lot will come down to the man's earning potential, which also rings true of Western women.

Many Western men find it confusing, but there are Indonesian women who accept money or gifts because they need to, or the opportunity is there. However, these women take care of their men wonderfully and they remain faithful. This may sound contradictory to what I wrote in the first chapter but Ankle's girlfriend was, it seems, a professional prostitute, and there is a distinction—the trick for men who take out Indonesian women from bars in Bali is to identify the difference.

It is my experience that a lot of relationships between Indonesian bargirls and their Western partners do not work. That said, when both parties take time to understand the cultural differences, some of them do. The first time I took an Indonesian girl home from a bar I was incredibly green about how things worked—not the sex side of it, that was easy—Indonesian women enjoy sex and they tend to be eager and willing partners, the problem is the idea of payment.

When I first arrived in Bali I came to think of it as The Land of Broken Men and I wasn't impressed. There were all these old guys who would sit in the pub all day, and they would crow about the twenty-year-old girl that they had slept with the night before. There was a boast to these conversations that didn't make sense to me. How could you brag about a woman you paid for, why would you want to? I had a hard time being subjected to these conversations and I would inevitably shut them down.

Morally it didn't appeal and as a sort of rebellion I became adamant that if I was going to take a woman home it would involve no exchange of sex for money. This was a naive way of thinking, as I would learn after I had lived in Bali for some time.

Unfortunately for me I am not the prettiest kid on the block and at this stage I lived in a dog box and rode around on a decrepit old motorbike. These are three very big strikes if you live in Indonesia and want to meet women.

Like most women, Indonesian women have a set of standards a man must comply with if they want to share their company: young and handsome is one, a good heart is another, but at the top of the tree is wealth and/or prospects. I would like to think I have a good heart, but unfortunately for me Meat Loaf never released a song entitled "One out of Three Ain't Bad".

I struggled. Quite simply, I did not want to pay and I could not afford to pay.

I found myself with a bit of a problem; everyone perceived

me to be a rich businessman but I never spent money and I often found myself being referred to as *pelit*. This means "skinny" in Indonesian and it refers to someone who is a tight arse. Despite this, I did achieve success in this endeavour a couple of months after I arrived.

One night I happened to be sitting in a bar with a mate when two gorgeous Indonesian girls walked in and sat across from us. My mate was in a relationship at the time so he wasn't interested. I on the other hand was chaffing at the bit, I had been trying my no cash policy for a while and wasn't having a great deal of success.

The girl I was checking out was incredibly beautiful; she had high cheek bones, a slim body and long silky black hair. She looked about twenty-seven—I was thirty-six—and as these things tend to go I started giving her the eye and she returned the favour. Things went on like this for a while until finally she said hello.

The girl and I were sitting a few metres apart, either side of a horseshoe-shaped bar, so the greeting was yelled across the open space between us.

I am a little shy when it comes to chatting up women. I can hold a conversation with anyone unless it is a girl I would like to sleep with ... put a pretty face in front of me and I clam up like an imbecile. I smiled, waved and said hello, then I went back to talking with my friend, anything to save me from having to sustain a conversation.

Again the girl took the lead. She introduced herself and her friend and then asked for my name. Being shy and afraid to talk, I called the barman over and passed him my phone with my number displayed. I then asked him to give it to the girl. My ploy worked. As soon as the barman returned my phone, the girl sent a message.

I felt I'd been very clever, I'd received the girl's number and I didn't have to say anything stupid. Now I could hold a conversation by text—a cop-out but also a great way to go for someone with a tendency to become lost for words.

I sent the girl a text with my name and I added one of those stupid smiley faces. Cool, right? I then carried on the conversation I was having with my friend. I ignored the girl for a while, long enough to feel she'd given up on me, then with little choice I screwed up my courage and I sent her a message asking if we could meet up later. Then I promptly got up and left the bar in case the girl wanted to talk!

The girl sent me a text half an hour later asking what I was up to. By this stage I had on a bit of a glow and I decided to try a little experiment. I don't know why I did this, maybe it was in the hope that the girl would get fed up and look elsewhere, but whenever the girl sent me a text, I would reply first with over-the-top kindness. "You're so beautiful, I can't wait to meet you." Then with the next text I would reply with over-the-top malice. "You're a working girl, I don't want anything to do with you."

This went on most of the night and surprisingly enough it worked—at the end of the evening the girl sent me a text that said she wanted to catch up. I sent the girl a message and told her to meet me at the pub where we'd met and I said that she was to jump on the back of my bike and that I didn't want to talk. I added that I would be taking her home and I wasn't going to pay for sex. The girl agreed.

I picked her up at the designated place and true to her word she jumped onto my bike without a word; we then rode to my place in silence.

The girl was beautiful and the sex was great. I was over the moon and very proud of my cunning plan. That was until her phone rang during an intense bout of lovemaking. She picked up her phone, looked at the number, motioned me to be quiet and answered.

The one-way conversation went something like this.

"Hello *sayang*."

"I miss you baby."

"Nothing baby, I'm just at home and about to go to sleep. I hope I dream of you darling."

"I love you so much baby."

The woman I was in the middle of having sex with was now whispering I love you to her boyfriend—talk about women multitasking. The conversation with the boyfriend went on for three or four minutes and I started to get bored. The girl happened to be sitting astride me and her titties were spectacular, but it's hard to stay focused when the women you're fucking is whispering sweet nothings to another man. I decided that even if her mind wasn't in it, I would go ahead and finish without her. I felt sorry for her boyfriend but I couldn't really pull out and un-fuck her.

However, I did have a plan. I decided I would finish what I had started but keep my conscience intact by concluding with a massive orgasmic groan. I hoped this would warn the boyfriend that his woman may not be totally kosher. I did my best to ignore the girl's conversation and I started to move rhythmically inside her, faster and faster.

This girl was talented, she didn't miss a beat. She placed a finger on my lips and warned me to remain quiet then she rode me like a rodeo queen without pause in her conversation. "Yes of course I love you baby, I will always be faithful to you."

She was a pro. Despite my best efforts, she managed to keep her voice composed and detached from what was happening beneath her. She also managed to see through my less-than-devious plan. Just as I was about to groan with pleasure she wound up her conversation. "OK, baby, I have to go now, this is costing you too much money. I'm tired, I love you baby, dream of me, goodbye."

Despite the setback I did manage to hold up my bargain to the brotherhood and moaned like a pornstar. Unfortunately I doubted my groan reached the ears of her boyfriend in England. The girl then hit me with her coup de grâce: she looked down at me, gave me her sweetest butter-wouldn't-melt-in-my-mouth smile and asked, "Do you think I'm stupid?"

This was actually the first conversation we'd had all night and I have to admit I felt somewhat beaten. "No," I replied limply, and then took the only revenge I could manage. I pushed her off me and promptly feel asleep.

When morning arrived, I was happy to see that my companion had stuck around and I was thinking we might go at it again but she had other ideas.

"Good morning," I said, and reached for her.

The girl pulled away. "Do you have money for me?"

I did my best to look surprised but the evening's phone call had allowed me a glimpse into her personality and I can't say that I was too shocked by the question. "I'm sorry sweetheart, but that wasn't the contract."

The girl pushed herself out of my bed and rolled to her feet. She then placed her hands on her fabulous naked hips. "Yes, but last night I was drunk and I thought you were handsome. Now I can see that you are ugly, you must give me money."

Not great for the ego, but brutality honest in true Indonesian fashion. Suffice to say, I didn't want to give her money after she had called me ugly, so I pulled up my blanket to cover my bruised ego. I placed an elbow on my pillow and, head in my hand, I did my best to look less ugly and replied. "But darling, you said no charge, you can't change the contract now."

The girl stamped a foot and everything jiggled. I don't know if she did this on purpose but the effect was somewhat moving.

"You must pay!" she hollered. "I have sex with you and I not like."

I felt like I had been doused with cold water and I realised morning sex was out of the question, she didn't seem up for it. Besides, being told I was ugly and bad in bed was not exactly a great aphrodisiac. I did however feel that the evening's activities should not be charged for. Business was business and the girl and I had made a verbal contract. "I'm sorry darling, but I will not give you money. Last night you say free, cannot change now."

She didn't look happy but to her credit she took it on the chin. She reached down to gather her clothes and started to pull them on. "OK, fuck you, I will go. Don't contact me again you fucking *pelit* ugly man. You fucking bad sex man!"

I watched her get dressed and felt a little hard done by. Unfortunately there was little I could do other than watch her tuck her beautiful body away. She collected her things and made to leave my room, but paused long enough to deliver another expletive and a few garbled Indonesian words, and then she stepped outside and slammed the door.

I found out later that she stole my motorbike helmet as payment.

I met her again about a month later. I happened to be riding down Legian Street when I noticed her walking alone. She noticed me too, flagged me down and, with no prompting on my part, she jumped on the back of my motorbike.

"Take me to your home," she demanded. I obeyed. The girl was stunning and maybe she had lied when she called me ugly and bad in bed.

Once inside, she dispensed with the niceties. "I need money, give me one hundred thousand and I will fuck you."

This was approximately ten Australian dollars, and it was cheap for a working girl in Bali. Had I known this at the time I may have taken her up on the offer. Unfortunately, I was probably still smarting from the ugly comment and the girl's demanding tone annoyed me. I don't like being told what to do.

"I don't pay," I told her.

She gave me a knowing smile. "Yes," she said "I think you will." She then took off all her clothes, lay down on my bed and, completely naked, stretched out gloriously in front of me. "I think you will pay me now," she purred.

I was green and still adamant that I wasn't going to pay for sex. This would all change in the not-too-distant future, but at the time it was how I felt. Besides, this woman had stolen my motorbike helmet and called me ugly. I wasn't going to be told that I had to give her money to have sex. I stood my ground and held onto my principles, then said the only thing I could think of to wound her. "You're not so beautiful," I declared, despite the fact that my eyes were devouring her lovely form.

The girl laughed at me and turned on her side. "You think?" she asked and smiled impishly. I knew I was beaten and had to change tack. I wracked my brain for a witty comeback. "Besides, you stole from me last time, why would I pay you this time?"

The girl covered herself with my pillow and gave me a wicked smile. "Your helmet was shit, why would I steal it?" I wanted to point out that she would only know my helmet was shit if she had in fact stolen it but it's not easy to argue with a beautiful naked woman.

"If you need money, why don't you call your boyfriend?" I shot back at her. I hoped this would cause her to have a yes-I-have-a-boyfriend-I-shouldn't-have-lied-to-you-I-should-fuck-you-for-free kind of reaction, but it wasn't to be. She reached over and pulled out her phone. "OK, I will call him," she said. She held a finger to her lips, "Be quiet, OK?"

"Hello darling, can you help me?"

I couldn't believe it. A month had passed and here I was with the same naked woman in my bed speaking to her boyfriend. This time I was adamant that I would send him a message.

I coughed. The girl shot me a foul look and said, "Yes of course darling, I miss you so much." I banged a glass down on the sink. She ignored me and giggled into the phone. "Yes baby, I also can't wait to see you." I opened a cupboard door and slammed it. The girl scowled at me. "No darling, I'm with my sister." I went into the toilet and pissed loudly, then flushed. From the bathroom I heard the girl plead poverty. "I have no money darling, I cannot eat." I walked to the fridge, grabbed a beer and sat down next to her. I then cracked the top of the Bintang, took a long swig and belched. The girl snarled silently then stood up and walked to the other side of the room, opened my curtains and looked outside. "I need some money, baby," she said. She was still naked and the light from the open window embraced her, making her look devastatingly sexy. I had had enough. I put my beer down and let rip a fart so loud that it could not possibly have emanated from her imaginary sister.

Too late. The girl closed the curtain, turned and smiled triumphantly at me. "My boyfriend will put money in my bank tonight, I will collect it in the morning. I don't need you, goodbye." Then she dressed and left.

I did the only thing a red-bloodied male in the situation could do. I followed her outside, picked up my new motorbike helmet and brought it inside. Then I walked to the pub and got drunk.

I did see the girl again but she would never talk or acknowledge me. She did however take great pleasure in parading men in front of me. I didn't mind, I had learned a lot about Indonesian women ... plus I'd shagged her and all it had cost me was an old motorbike helmet.

Sour Chocolate

Naked phone girl taught me a useful lesson involving Indonesian women, but not all Indonesian women are like this. I had met the girl in a pub off the strip and that should have been an indication that she wasn't working but it is sometimes hard to tell. An Indonesian girl you meet in a big nightclub in Kuta will almost always be a hooker. A girl you meet working behind a bar, on the other hand, is usually not on the game and may not be interested in foreign men at all. I have seen many tourists walk into a bar and treat the girl behind the counter like she is a working girl. The poor girl is probably pulling twelve-hour shifts and working six days a week; all she wants to do is to go home and spend her one day off with her Indonesian boyfriend.

A lot of the time these girls take revenge for this unfair treatment by accepting gifts from men, and why shouldn't they? I know if someone treated me like a commodity, I would. Unfortunately this often leaves the guy bitter and the girl thinking all Western men are pigs with money.

A simple way around this is to chat to the girl and ask if she is in a relationship—she will generally be straight up.

Indonesians girls are very forthright and they will ask the question themselves, they will also prompt a man to ask them by posing the same questions. Are you married? Do you have a girlfriend? This can be misinterpreted as a come-on but what they are saying is, "ask me if I have one" then things can be placed on an even playing field and the guy will find he is given a level of respect.

More than once I have been warned of danger or told to avoid a particular person by a girl who works behind a bar, simply because I enquired about her background and was then able to afford her the level of respect she deserved. A good example of this is a girl I met called Lovi. The name says it all; Lovi was sweet, funny, smart and an all-round nice person. I fell madly in love with her.

Lovi worked at a Chinese restaurant quite some distance from my place. I just happened to pop in for a drink one day and the girl that came out to serve me instantly caught my eye. Lovi was about twenty-six or twenty-seven; she had long curly hair, a stunning smile and an infectious laugh. I did all I could to get her to go out with me.

Lovi was from Sumatra and had just arrived in Bali so she was a little shy and didn't have a wide circle of friends; I was in the same boat. She was also a Christian and would go to church every Sunday. She had once even dreamt of becoming a nun. For some reason that I have never delved into this appealed to me, perhaps an analysis of this would be better left to a psychiatrist.

I would go to meet Lovi at her restaurant any chance that I could get and I would try and work out a way to ask her out. Eventually, after at least six months, I came up with a plan that probably sounds foolish but as I have said when it comes to women I am eternally shy and a little stupid. One day, while chatting, I mentioned that I had to go back to Australia for a short stint and I asked if she would like me to bring her anything. Lovi asked me to bring her a koala, a real one, and then a kangaroo. When I told her I couldn't she feigned disappointment and settled on some Australian chocolate.

I told Lovi I would bring her the chocolate, but I mentioned if I did she would have to come to dinner with me. She told me she would think about it and the two weeks I spent in Australia felt like the longest stretch I had ever endured. To cut a long story short, when I returned to Bali I delivered Lovi's chocolate and she said that she would come out with me. Unfortunately, she said something along the lines of, "why not, you're the best one."

Obviously this got me thinking I was not the only suitor and when I called her to go out she didn't answer my first two attempts so I sent her a nasty message along the lines of "fuck you". Very smooth, even I say so myself. Lovi then called me a few minutes later and told me that she didn't answer because she was talking to her sister who had just given birth to her first child, and then she cancelled our date. Eventually Lovi met another guy and they are now married. I wish her nothing but luck, but again I learnt a lesson: don't tell the girl you are in love with to go fuck herself.

About three months after I met Lovi she introduced me to a friend of hers, Shia. Shia was a fourteen-year-old Balinese runaway who lived in the room beneath Lovi; apparently her father used to beat her and she had been left with no choice but to get away from the family home.

She had taken a shine to Lovi. I knew this because she wore

a Christian cross similar to the one Lovi wore, and this is very unusual for a Balinese Hindu girl. When I enquired about the cross, Lovi explained that she was doing her best to look after Shia, teach her English and help find her a good job. Shia in turn had come to see Lovi as an older sister and protector, so she wore the cross as sign of her dedication to Lovi. She had also started accompanying Lovi to Mass every Sunday. Every time I meet with Lovi, Shia would be at her side, she would say hello, then sit quietly and do her best to follow the conversation. She did this to better her English, she was a sweet kid and I took a shine to her.

One afternoon, Lovi, Shia and I were sitting at the table when a seedy Balinese guy of about thirty-five walked across the road and sat down with us. I knew something wasn't quite right because Lovi became uncomfortable. Shia on the other hand beamed. Uncertain what was taking place I introduced myself and started a conversation. The newcomer introduced himself as Wowan and began touting for the tattoo shop across the road. This was expected and although I wasn't interested I listened to what he had to say.

Wowan carried on about the shop for a while and then as he was speaking he reached under the table and placed a hand on Shia's leg. He must have noticed my look because his shop talk suddenly dried up. Wowan smiled showing me his nicotine stained teeth. "What?" he asked. "Do you have problem?"

I hadn't liked the look of Wowan to begin with; he was skinny and tattooed and he had the eyes of a snake. I cringed at the idea of him placing his hand on the young girl's leg. "Do you know Shia?" I asked him, trying to keep the indignation out of my voice.

Wowan laughed, his eye's hooded over. "What has it got to do with you?" he asked.

I tried to err on the side of caution. A hand on the leg didn't necessarily mean anything I told myself, the Balinese have a different perspective when it comes to touching. "It has nothing to do with me," I said, "I'm curious because Shia is a friend of Lovi's."

Wowan hissed laughter. "She's also a friend of mine," he said, then winked in a way that left me in no doubt about their relationship.

I paused to take in what Wowan had said. I could feel the anger and bile rise up in my throat. I felt protective over Shia and I couldn't help but think that if a man said the same thing to me in Australia I would have done all I could to inflict some kind of hurt on him. I also knew I had to be careful, I wasn't in Australia and I had been warned on numerous occasions not to attack an Indonesian. I took a deep breath and tried to control my temper. "You do know she's fourteen?"

Wowan giggled. He lifted his arm and draped it about Shia's shoulder. "What you think, I'm stupid?"

I took a mouthful of beer, swallowed and placed my bottle gently on the table. "She's fourteen," I said again and smiled, "and no, I don't think you're stupid."

Wowan smiled back, then looked over at Shia. "I know she's fourteen," he said. "She's my sweet chocolate." He ran a finger lightly down Shia's cheek and brushed a piece of hair from her forehead.

I clenched my jaw, fought my anger, leaned forward against

the table, and squared my shoulders. "You make joke, ya?" I asked him.

Wowan laughed in my face, he gave Shia a peck on the cheek and she smiled. I watched as his hand moved up and down the young girl's waist. "I not make joke about my sweet, sweet chocolate."

I couldn't help myself. I leaned forward and glared at Wowan. "You should be careful, ya."

I felt Lovi's hand grab the back of my shirt and she gently pulled me back into my seat. "Leave it, Mal," she whispered.

Wowan held my eyes, he put his hand back under the table and gave Shia's leg another squeeze. Shia giggled. "Do you like sweet chocolate?" he asked me and smiled.

"What do you mean?" I replied and I heard my voice break. Emotion had got the better of me. I coughed to clear my throat and took a moment to control myself. "What are you trying to say?" I managed through clenched teeth.

Wowan laughed. It had a false and flinty ring to it that put my nerves on edge. "What do you think I mean?" he said and leaned forward to stare at me, "she's my girlfriend, my sweet chocolate. Maybe you want some of my sweet chocolate?"

I reminded myself that it was not smart to attack an Indonesian and I fought myself not to react but I couldn't help myself. "Fuck you," I uttered.

Wowan snickered, goaded me, "sweet, sweet chocolate". He rocked his body, started to sing. He placed his arm back around Shia's shoulder and pulled her close.

I pushed myself back in the chair. I was too angry to formulate words and I knew I was seconds away from flying over the table and grabbing the seedy bastard by the throat. As I started to rise, Lovi stopped me. She clamped her hand down on my leg, then reached over and placed her other hand on my chin. She turned me to face her, pushing me into my chair with her eyes. "No," she said firmly. Lovi waited, watched me settle, then she turned to Shia and spoke in blistering Indonesian.

Shia got up from the table and left without a word. Lovi then turned her attention to Wowan and let fly with angry Indonesian words and aggressive hand gestures. I didn't know what was said but the two of them became involved in a heated argument. The argument went back and forth until Wowan suddenly stopped talking. An uncomfortable hush settled over the table. Wowan stared at Lovi and I watched as his eyes filled with hatred. Lovi held her ground, she clenched her fists and bared her perfect white teeth.

I was ready to jump in if he tried to hurt her, but I needn't have worried. A brief glimpse at Lovi's eyes showed me the full force of her Sumatran anger. I had no doubt she would have hurt Wowan far worse than I could have if he'd tried anything.

Wowan tried to stare Lovi down but then he yielded. He pushed his chair back, got up from the table and stormed back across the road.

When Wowan had gone back to wherever he had crawled out of, I turned to Lovi and asked what had happened. I could see she was still angry, but she explained that Wowan belonged to that corner and that he was thirty-six and married with three children. She said that he was part of a group that touted for the tattoo shop across the road and that, if I had attacked him they would all have joined in the fight.

She said that Wowan had been hanging around Shia since she'd arrived and that he had taken her out and got her drunk a few times. She said that Shia looked up to him and that yes, they were sleeping together. Lovi told me that she was doing her best to keep Wowan away from Shia, hence they went to Church, but that she had no real power over him because he was Balinese and she was Sumatran and new to Bali. She then told me that the only reason Wowan had got up and left is that she threatened to tell her boss that he was disturbing customers, namely me. She said that I would be safe around the restaurant but that I should be careful if I ever met Wowan in another place.

Shia was around a few times after the incident but one day she disappeared. When I enquired about her, Lovi told me she was gone. I asked her if she had returned to her home, but she said she didn't know. Kuta is no place for a homeless fourteen-year-old girl.

You may be wondering why Lovi and I didn't go to the police, there is of course an age of consent in Indonesia. I'm a foreigner and if I accused a Balinese of doing something to another Indonesian the Polisi would have laughed in my face and charged me for the privilege.

Lovi was a waitress in a restaurant and for her this would have been pointless, dangerous and expensive. It also goes against the way Indonesians think, they do not involve the police as it's too expensive.

Smoke and Mirrors

Despite what many may think, the Balinese run Bali and they have no great love for their Indonesian cousins. Asli Bali (original Bali) is all that matters. If the Balinese had their way, anyone who was not Balinese would be out and that includes Westerners. Different Indonesian societies tend to distrust each other so the Javanese, Sumatrans, Lombokians, etc display no great affection for the Balinese but, understandably, they distrust Westerners the most.

Do not be fooled when a Balinese tells you that it is the Javanese who rip everyone off in Bali. The Balinese stick their fingers into the tourist pie as much as anybody. I hear this all the time from Westerners and it annoys me. A lot of tourists trot this out as way of showing they understand Bali.

"Watch out for the Javanese, my wallet was stolen but there were too many of them, the Javanese are all criminals." This is in fact a falsehood spread by the Balinese that is designed to vilify the Javanese and clear all Balinese of any wrongdoing. I instantly think any Westerner that says this to me is naive. The Balinese in general have a tendency to blame somebody else if things go wrong (and when they run out of people, they blame ghosts or gods). I have seen the Balinese pull as many scams as the Javanese, the Balinese are just better at the blame game.

The Javanese consider the Balinese to be stupid, while the Balinese consider the Javanese to be criminals. Amongst most Indonesians the Javanese are considered very hard workers while the Balinese are considered lazy—logic would dictate that it is the lazy person who becomes a thief, but of course this is a generalisation.

The first time I came to Bali was in the late Eighties. I was twenty at the time and I came for a two-week holiday with a girlfriend. While sitting on Kuta Beach I had a run-in with a Balinese beach vendor because I would not buy his product and the gentleman then threatened me with a knife. This happened more than twenty years ago and all though I may have been an obnoxious tourist, I certainly did not do anything worthy of being stabbed.

The fact that things like this have been happening in Bali for such a long period is beyond me, the fact that Bali wins the best tropical holiday destination year after year when things like this happen is astounding. The only thing I can put this down to is the Balinese habit of blaming anybody but themselves. Balinese are experts at employing the smoke and mirrors tactic and they use it all the time.

On numerous occasions I have witnessed Balinese in full ceremonial dress pull up at the seafront in a flatbed truck fully laden with rubbish from a ceremony then dump it in the ocean. Recently an article appeared in *Time* magazine entitled: "My Holiday Hell". The article highlighted the problems Kuta Beach had with rubbish, amongst other things, and it caused a bit of a stir on the island.

A Balinese regent and spokesman in charge of rubbish collection came out and released a statement to the press in which he claimed the rubbish problems on Kuta Beach were not the fault of the Balinese. This rebuttal to the *Time* article was entitled "Kuta Merely Victim of Wind-Blown Rubbish: Regent". In the article, the Balinese regent was quoted as saying that *"This rubbish that is washing up at Kuta Beach is all from outside Bali. Nothing is locally produced; it's all from outside Kuta. Kuta is just a victim ... For example, we all know there are no forests in Bali, but the rubbish that washes up in Kuta includes logs. Also, there's lots of plastic that certainly didn't originate in Kuta ... we also hope that Indonesians outside of Bali will stop throwing their rubbish into the sea and making Kuta a victim."*

This is the Balinese mindset, it is also perhaps why Balinese never seem to be taken to task for what happens in Bali. Far from what the Balinese like to present to the outside world, all the criminals in Bali are not Javanese. There are good, honest and kind people from all over Indonesia who live in Bali. There are also good, honest and kind Balinese people, but they are not the problem. The problem is that misdeeds are often expertly hidden or passed off as somebody else's responsibility.

Unfortunately a lot of tourists swallow the hype presented in travel guides that the Balinese are a peaceful, spiritual race of people without a bad bone in their bodies. This is just not true. There is good and bad in any society.

From Paris with Love

I first learnt the simple truth that good and bad exists in every society from a prostitute who used to visit me a long time ago, but I would experience it in many forms during my time in Bali. This prostitute was a real piece of work and well known about town. I had a soft spot for this woman and she hung around until one fateful day when I just couldn't take it anymore.

I had given up my policy of no payment for sex after two years. I had tried my best but as they say man doesn't live by bread alone and I was finding semi-celibacy hard to take. If I had to justify this, and I'm not sure I do, I would say that I came to Bali to work, not for the illicit nightlife, but somehow I became ensnared.

Unfortunately, prostitution in all its forms is almost considered a way of life for men and women in certain segments of Balinese society. I was stuck in a less salubrious part of the island and I would be for the next few years. To avoid prostitution was to remain home, alone, single and celibate. I was given a choice, live like a saint or become a sinner, and for better or worse I chose the latter.

What I liked about this particular woman was that despite being one of the better-known hookers in town she was brutally honest about it. I think she simply had no reason to lie to herself or anyone else. This suited me at the time. I had no wish to corrupt a poor local girl with my white man's money (or lack of). This woman had been corrupted long before I arrived on the scene, she was a bad as they come. I guess this eased my conscious— she knew she was a prostitute and she didn't care what anybody thought. She was as willing to take from me as I was from her.

This woman had a mouth on her that never stopped. She cursed worse than me, drank more than me and was a lot nastier than me. She had a scorpion tattooed on her thigh and it suited her. She also dyed her hair blonde and idolised Paris Hilton. For this story I'll call her Paris, she would enjoy it.

I met Paris on the beach one day. She was with a customer and was demanding that he pay to get her nails done. The customer was cowering under Paris's tongue and she was enjoying the crowd watch her rip into him. It was funny and I was laughing along with the rest of the people sitting around. Paris was being a vicious bitch and the poor guy was not only embarrassed that the woman he was with looked so much like a hooker but was also embarrassed that she was treating him like an Idiot Westerner who would hang out with a hooker.

Paris noticed me watching and when the customer got up to buy her something, we exchanged a few words. She asked where I was from and where I lived. "Australia and Seminyak," I replied flippantly. I actually lived in a small, sparse hotel room in Kuta, but I had learned it was better to keep my address a secret. She smiled when I said I lived in Seminyak and I should have taken the hint. When her client returned with her gift, Paris went back and sat beside him and resumed her abuse.

The next time I saw Paris was as at a well-known pick-up spot in Kuta. I would find out later that she hung out all the time but it didn't bother me, she was what she was and I was looking for company. I entered the club, walked over to the bar and ordered a drink. Paris noticed me and promenaded over. She had a walk on her that screamed, "I'm a hooker and proud of it". I loved the honesty in that strut, and decided to take her home. She marched up in her high heels and mini skirt, placed a hand on my shoulder and introduced herself. "I know you, we met on the beach. I noticed you looking at me, buy me a drink."

I refused. I had just arrived at the club and I had a budget, so, despite my attraction, I wasn't about to be told that I had to buy a drink from the first girl that came up to me. "No thank you," I said, and turned away from her and went back to cradling my beer by the bar.

Paris smiled and laughed knowingly. "You will buy me a drink," she said and then she walked off into the crowd.

I wasn't certain Paris would return but I was willing to take my chances. I waved her goodbye, turned my back on the bar and settled in to watch the throng of drunken tourists cavorting around the club. She returned ten minutes later with a man in tow. The guy looked like a tourist of the European variety. He was well dressed and handsome in a parted-blonde-hair kind of way. He ordered Paris a drink and she gave me a smart-arse smile.

I ignored her and her would-be companion. I was uncomfortable so I scanned the crowd and tried hard to look like I was scanning the crowd. Paris accepted a colourful drink from the milk-toothed tourist then she turned her back on him, tapped me on the shoulder and said, "Hello." She then lifted her cocktail to her brightly coloured lips, took a sip and looked at me over the rim of her glass waiting for me to reply.

I took a good look at her. She was sexy in a painted-up-prostitute kind of way. Pointing to her companion with my eyes, I asked, "What about him?"

Paris trickled laughter and poked at the ice in her cocktail glass. "I'm not interested in him, I'm interested in you. He's here to get you jealous and ..." Paris held up her drink like a pro "... to buy me this."

I looked over at Paris's companion. He seemed nervous. I could tell he was uncomfortable with the scene and with my presence. I told Paris I didn't care about her companion and I was certainly not jealous. "Stay with him if you like. Have another drink, you will be coming home with me," I said with a confidence that only comes with alcohol.

Paris smiled, flicked her hair then placed an arm about my waist. "I knew you wanted me," she said happily. The milk-toothed tourist fled the scene and Paris and I finished our drinks and walked out of the club together.

When we arrived at my home I could see Paris was disappointed. Seminyak residents are considered wealthy and I lived in Kuta and had unintentionally conned her on the beach.

She walked inside, dumped her purse on a table, turned to me and said, "Your house is shit. You live in Kuta and Kuta is shit." Then she tore into me about my living conditions.

I ignored her and got myself a drink, sat on the bed, and let her ramble on for a few moments. When I'd had enough I said, "Fuck off and find somebody else, I'm sure your little friend with the blonde hairdo will take you home."

She thought about it for a moment, then walked to my bar fridge and pulled out a Mix Max vodka mix. She opened the drink and sat on the bed next to me. "You're very lucky. Normally I wouldn't sleep with you," she said. I don't know why but I found her nastiness intriguing and funny. Perhaps in the same way you might find it intriguing and funny to put a scorpion in your bed, and after our first night together I knew I would keep Paris around for a while.

In the end we had sex, I paid and she left. It should have been a perfect relationship by Kuta standards, but it didn't end there. We started a nasty boots and all relationship, and yes, of course, it did sometimes involve payment, but the sex was good and I enjoyed the repartee. She would visit about once a week, she would start to complain and I would threaten to kick her out. And then we would fall into bed and have crazy sex.

Paris was a bitch but she had a deep respect for money, so every time she came to visit she would complain about the security at my hotel.

"Fucking Balinese. I hate the fucking Balinese," she would say as she stormed through my door, threwing her clothes on my bed and helping herself to the contents of my fridge. I was intrigued. I thought the Balinese were wonderful people who were above doing anybody harm so I asked her why she hated the Balinese so much.

The hotel where I lived was owned and staffed by Balinese;

this meant the security were also Balinese. The problem was that the Balinese security would not let Paris into the hotel complex unless she paid them, and the problem we had with this was that I did not always pay Paris. We'd got to know each other over a period of time and for whatever reason we enjoyed each other's company. Paris would ask for money if she needed it, but on many occasions she let it slide. The security would not take this as an excuse however; they expected Paris to pay a fine anytime she came to my hotel.

I wasn't happy with this situation and I took to meeting Paris at the front gate and walking her out when she left. This solved the problem to some extent but after more discussion with Paris I learned the practice was rife throughout Bali.

Anyone working in Bali who is not from Bali, including prostitutes, must carry an identification card, and when a person is found working without one of these cards they are imprisoned by the local Balinese Banjar. They will remain incarcerated until they come up with an acceptable bribe. Unless a prostitute is with her client, security at most hotels will ask for this card when a prostitute tries to enter, to get her card back the prostitute then has to share her takings with the security.

Security in Bali is therefore a very lucrative job and the Balinese keep a very tight rein on it. There are frequent brutal and violent power struggles over security positions that tourists don't see. A lot of these battles stem from the clubs, but I have heard of them happening in the hotel environment. Most security at the hotels and nightclubs are Balinese and most working girls are Javanese or at least from outside Bali—this is slowly changing on both sides but mainly it's still the case. These Javanese working girls are exploited ruthlessly by Balinese security.

Girls Just Want to Have Fun

An interesting phenomenon, which was recently exposed in the fascinating film documentary "Cowboys in Paradise", is the large number of Western and Japanese women who come to Bali seeking the attention of young men, both Western and Indonesian. Some of these women seem to have a bee in their bonnet about Western men living in Southeast Asia but they believe their own actions are beyond reproach.

I was once accused of paying Indonesian girls for sex by a forty-year-old Western woman who was sleeping with male Western tourists in their twenties. This accusation was levelled at me while we were sitting in a large group of people and for no other reason than because I lived in Bali. I was still in my no-payment phase but my accuser refused to accept this.

On another occasion, a forty-two-year-old Australian divorcee boasted to me about her latest conquest: a nineteen-year-old Western boy. I didn't judge her but I did make a note of the fact that she complained about Western men dating younger Indonesian girls.

On yet another occasion a Western woman, who had booked a friend's villa, rang all her friends and stated she would not stay in the house because the owner was sleeping with children. She claimed the victim was a child when in fact she was twenty-six, she was the owner's long-time girlfriend and she had a five-year-old son from a previous marriage. Obviously the accusation hurt this man's reputation and his business.

I have met Western women who come to Bali for two weeks, pick up a different bloke every night, and then go home to their families to play wife and mum. This seems to happen on a rotational basis and the two-week girl's holiday away from hubby and the kids is generally an organised triple-S tour: shop, spa and sex.

Female tourists also love young Indonesian boys. They pick them up, pay all their bills and buy them clothes, drinks and food. For whatever reason, a lot of these women see this as normal; they are just helping the poorer partner in the relationship keep up. That is until a man does the same thing. This they term as prostitution.

Surprisingly this is most prevalent among Japanese women, who seem to love Indonesian boys, and you often see a beautiful young Japanese girl traipsing around with her Indonesian boyfriend. As for the older Japanese women they are somewhat careful about these liaisons and they are generally carried out behind closed doors.

I was told once that this is a dominance thing. Japanese girls are given very little respect or power in their country, and creating a relationship with an Indonesian and controlling the finances allows them a level of power that they would otherwise not receive. I was told this by one of the legendary Kuta cowboys, Bali's beach gigolos. The guy that told me this has gone as far as marrying two Western women and living in Australia with both, and he also has a child with a Japanese girl. He has since given up this lifestyle and wants to marry an Indonesian girl.

For Western women this happens more than most people would believe, and although it has been going on for a long time Western women are now becoming a little more blasé in these endeavours. I have no problem with this, but it can be a case of glass houses, especially when I hear the problems Indonesian women have with Western women when they try and settle down with their Western men in a place like Australia.

The other thing about Western women that surprises me is that they attempt to pick up Indonesian working girls. Only recently, a friend's Indonesian girlfriend told me that two Western women had tried to pick her up in a nightclub. This was not the first time I had heard of this and a lot of working girls have had similar experiences. Timi, a girl I know who works as a masseuse, tells me that Western women often ask for happy endings. Timi works in an upmarket, supposedly legitimate, spa; the place is exclusively for women and Timi studied hard to get the job so she did not have to give happy endings to men. I questioned Timi relentlessly about this and she swore that it was true and that it was happening in spas all over Bali.

Personally I couldn't give a toss what female tourists get up to; I only mention it because male tourists get such a bad rap.

He is Heavy
and He's not My Brother

Living in Bali can break a lot of people. I don't know if this is
exclusively Bali's fault, or if a large majority of people who come
to Bali to start new lives are already wounded, but I have seen a
lot of people pushed to the verge of a breakdown and their plans
for a new life in tatters.

A good friend of mine who came to live in Bali resorted to
stealing money when things got tight and he was found crying
in a corner when caught. Another friend ended up delivering
restaurant food for the equivalent of two dollars a delivery after
he lost his house and all the money in his bank accounts. He was
sixty years old, fell in love with the wrong girl and trusted the
wrong Indonesian. He lost his life savings and without enough
money to fly home he eked out a life living like a local.

The stories of expats who have lost everything are numerous
and a lot of these people spend their time wandering the streets
of Bali like lost souls. Sometimes somebody will step in to
help, which unfortunately, for the most part, leads to the Good
Samaritan being stung. The person who stole the money and cried
about it went on to steal from my family when we helped him.

Lesson learned. As for my friend who got a job delivering food, I would have loved to fly him home but there was no way I could afford it. If I bailed out every person who was broke in Bali I would be bankrupt as well. Sometimes all you can do is buy them a beer and a feed, give them some words of encouragement and be on your way. This may sound harsh but the reality is that in Bali it's the survival of the fittest.

One friend told me the story of a mate who went with his young bride to live in Java and on arriving at their new home, which he had paid for, he was told that the girl's three brothers were going to move in. This worked for about a month until the brothers decided to confiscate the guy's passport and bank cards. They then held him to ransom and forced him to become their personal slave. He was given a small room at the back of the house, was beaten, made to clean up after everyone and was forced to fetch food and alcohol that was paid for from his accounts. This may sound like a case of a stupid older man falling in love with a younger woman and, of course, it was. The man in question was in his late fifties and the woman in her late twenties, but by all reports he was a nice guy who wanted to give the girl some kind of life.

The girl was a prostitute who had been selling herself around Bali for years; he apparently felt that he could help her and her family by moving with her to Java. Eventually this guy managed to get word to a few friends and three of them flew to Java to retrieve him. They applied enough pressure to get the passport returned but unfortunately the bank accounts had been emptied so the friends flew him back to Bali at their own expense. Sadly he died shortly after his return. Then, because he had been broke and had no relatives, the three friends had to pay for his burial.

This is just another Bali hard-luck story and there are thousands of them. I sat in a pub one night with a young guy who had just experienced the same thing. He was twenty years old and had gone to Java on an exchange program, but when he arrived in Java his passport and belongings were confiscated. The young guy managed to escape after a month but as he regaled his story he broke down and sobbed; he flew home to his family the next day.

These stories are Java based and Bali is a little less isolated but Westerners get themselves into trouble here all the time. One of the main problems Westerners have is they believe their safety is secured by their generosity. Recently a friend told me that he didn't expect any problems in Bali and he didn't need to be careful because he had a local tough watching his back. I inquired as to how he had achieved this.

"Whenever I see Abraham I buy him a beer, no one's going to fuck with me while I have him in my corner."

Abraham is a five-foot-nothing local guy who is missing a lot of teeth, has a reputation for being connected, has apparently spent time in jail and is often seen carrying a knife; he is also a little past it and is something of a sad character who has a drinking problem. He does project a sense of danger, but, I have no doubt Abraham wouldn't care less that some rich white person brought him a beer if trouble started.

Westerners often fall into this trap. There is a saying that money doesn't buy you love. It does in Indonesia; the problem is the measure of the love your money buys. Loyalty, friendship and love are commodities in Indonesia, but what many don't realise is they are traded on a rental basis—the contract is valid while you pay, if the money dries up so does the service.

Another trap is the family association. I now try and avoid contact with any person who tells me they have "Indonesian family". I don't know how many times I have had the conversation but I have grown bored of trying to explain to disbelieving Westerners that their Indonesian family may not be all that they seem. What is more likely is that the Indonesian family sees the association as a business opportunity. A typical conversation may unfold like this:

"They're my brother/sister/family, and they will always look after me. They have never asked for money."

"Why are they your family?"

"I get invited to all their ceremonies, I even went to their daughter's wedding."

"Did you take a present?"

"No, I was told that most people give money so I put a few hundred dollars in an envelope and gave it to the bride's mother."

"OK, as I understand it this is common practise at some weddings, but do you think you may have been invited because you are a rich Westerner and your gift is probably going to be larger than most?"

"My family wouldn't do that to me, I have known them for years. I have been coming to Bali for two weeks a year for the past six years, and I met them on my first trip up here."

"So in effect you have known them for twelve weeks, that is if

you spent every day with them while you were here."

"Well that isn't entirely true, I have called them from time to time, and they send me a text message every now and again."

"Oh that's nice, did they ask for anything when they sent you a text?"

"They had a few problems, one of their children got sick so I helped out, that's what families do and they help me every time I come to Bali."

"I can understand that, nobody likes to hear that a child is sick and hospital treatment is expensive in Bali. I guess you sent some money right?"

"Yes, but only a little, just enough to get the child medical treatment."

"Fair enough, I think it is a nice thing to do. Before you said your family helps every time you come to Bali?"

"Oh they're great. If I ever need to hire a car, or to book a tour, or to organise a hotel room, I just give them a call and they get the whole thing sorted."

"That's nice of them; did you know that most bookings in Bali run on a commission basis? But your family probably doesn't take commission when they book things for you, right?"

"I don't know, I doubt it, they wouldn't do that, I helped pay for their son when he was sick and I'm putting their daughter through school. My family is also thinking of bringing the children to Australia next year."

"OK, so this makes you family, seems to me you give them money though?"

"I have never given them money unless it was important, you

can't call putting a kid in school is giving someone money; would you call buying the family a motorbike so their daughter can get to school, giving money?"

"Yeah sort of, you bought the family a motorbike?"

"I really trust them. They have nothing and they would give anything to me; plus they have never asked for money, it's just she needed a motorbike to get to school. They're also going to use it for the family business."

"The family has a business?"

"They have a few cars they rent out; they own a small tour company."

"How much was the motorbike?"

"I brought a brand new Mio, it only cost twenty million and they gave me receipts.

"Strange, a brand new Mio costs thirteen million."

"No it doesn't, I checked the receipt."

"Was the receipt book written in Indonesian?"

"Yes."

"Did you know you can buy a receipt book in Bali for about five thousand Rupiah?"

"No."

"Did you know that for about one hundred thousand you can get any person anywhere to put whatever price you want on whatever receipt you get?"

"They wouldn't do that, they are my family."

It's about this point that I give up, especially when the subject matter is some bloke's wife or "my Balinese brother".

Just the other day it was reported in a local paper that two Westerners were sent to jail because they defrauded another Westerner of US$195,000. The victim transferred her money as a deposit on some land to a business partner of the Westerners—the business partner was Indonesian and the money was sent to his bank account. It soon came to light that the land was not owned by the Westerners or the Indonesian and that the Indonesian partner had disappeared with all the money.

What I found amusing about this story was that one of the Westerners was named Angus. The Indonesian partner was also named Angus. I'm just guessing but Angus is not a common Indonesian name and the coincidence of a Westerner and an Indonesian named Angus going into business together is somewhat unlikely. My guess would be that Angus the Indonesian changed his name so that he and Angus the Westerner could be brothers. I would also like to bet that Angus the Westerner was chuffed at this—so chuffed that he trusted his Indonesian brother to secure land, do all his legals and open a bank account that money could be transferred into.

Why wouldn't he? Angus the Indonesian had changed his name and you have to trust a person that has changed his name to your own, don't you?

Shame that the land was never purchased and that all the money and the Indonesian once known as Angus soon disappeared. I wonder what Angus the Westerner now thinks as he sits in Kerobokan Jail. I also wonder if Angus the Indonesian ever changed his name back.

There are of course exceptions to these rules but I haven't

come across many. I have also been caught before, as has anyone who has lived in Indonesia, and I am very lucky that I was given advice when I arrived in Bali by people who had spent a long time in Indonesia.

Many Balinese traps do not involve the locals at all but unscrupulous expats. A great deal of people get caught up in dodgy business scams. Bali is a tough town full of crooked people trying to make a buck.

About two weeks ago I had a beer with a guy who I had just met. He seemed like a nice bloke at the time but two days ago I heard the same guy had pulled a scam for US$100,000 and had fled the country.

Things like this happen all the time here. One hundred thousand dollars is a lot of money in Southeast Asia. Southeast Asia is also an easy place to get lost in when you have that kind of money. I heard about the rip-off from a friend of mine who happened to associate with both people involved. At the time we were sitting in an expat bar and the scam was the topic of conversation. My friend was filling me in on the finer details as the conversation flowed amongst the other expats. While we talked, the guy who had been fleeced walked in and everything went quiet.

The victim of the scam must have realised he'd been the topic of conversation and after a brief moment he brought up the uncomfortable situation. The bar then discussed the scam openly until my friend piped up with a bit of information that stopped the conversation dead in its tracks—he told the bar that he was still in touch with the scam artist by email and that he had received mail earlier that day. The victim was shocked; he asked my friend if he knew this perpetrator's whereabouts and the content of the email.

My friend explained that the email he'd received had contained little more than a hello, but he volunteered to contact the guy there and then and he retrieved his laptop from his car. After a brief discussion an email was sent stating plainly that my friend was sitting in a bar with the victim and that he would like to get in touch.

"Do you have anything to say?" it asked.

No one at the bar thought this would work but almost instantly we received a reply. My friend opened the email. "A man's got to do, what a man's got to do," it said simply. The victim was livid and more emails were sent. Unfortunately no further replies were received and after a while he left. As soon as he'd gone the jokes started.

What struck me most about this scenario was that the guy who had pulled the scam had no remorse and the people in the bar had no sympathy. Most found the perpetrator's reply funny.

The Demise of an English Rose

Some of the first people I met when I came to live in Bali were a couple called Mick and Tracy. The couple had met in the UK through a dating service and they had sold up what they owned and come to Bali to start a new life and business together. I knew Mick and Tracy well enough to have a beer once in a while but didn't consider myself close. The couple were English, as were most of their friends, and they seemed reluctant to allow an Australian into their circle. Mick and Tracy did what a lot of people do when they come to Bali: they opened a small restaurant-cum-bar, and despite the odds they were reasonably successful.

Things went well for the couple until for whatever reason they decided to break up and go their separate ways. Mick continued to run the restaurant and he seemed unfazed by the separation. It was easy to see that he'd instigated the split. Tracy on the other hand was heartbroken and she spent the next month traipsing around Bali in a filthy state of drunken desperation.

Most people have faced an emotional low period at some stage of their lives and generally with the help of family or friends they manage to drag themselves up and move on, but sometimes people publically fall to such a level that they are noticeably in need of help. This is was what happened to Tracy. The once bubbly English redhead transformed into a broken pitiful drunk in a matter of weeks.

I would often see Tracy as she stumbled from bar to bar. She was dirty and unkempt, her hair was a matted mess and the makeup she wore was a grime-filled swamp on her face. Sadly, everyone loves a train wreck, and a thirty-year-old English woman roaming Bali's streets covered in her own vomit was, to some, a great source of mirth.

I watched Tracy's demise from a distance. I'd had little contact with the couple for some time, and was only an acquaintance, but I felt that Mick or someone within the couple's circle had an obligation to help her. Unfortunately I was given no choice in the matter. One day, at about three in the morning, Tracy turned up on my balcony. I woke to hear a banging on my door. Tracy was drunk and could barely stand, but she begged to be let in and asked me for help through the closed door.

I had no idea why Tracy chose my door and I didn't want to get involved. As far as I was concerned Tracy was somebody else's problem so I ignored the ruckus and pretended to be asleep. Tracy eventually fell asleep on my doorstep. I checked on her every now and then and I placed a blanket over her and a pillow under her head. Later that morning she moved on.

The following night I was in a bar with a group of friends and another of my brothers, Jack. Jack was on holiday and I was showing him around. We were catching up and enjoying a quiet beer when Tracy entered the bar.

She looked dishevelled and dirty, she wore the same dress I'd seen her in the night before and it was covered in vomit stains.

Tracy lurched over to Jack and me and she started to scold me for not letting her into my room the night before. I felt embarrassed. To anyone watching, including my brother, it would have appeared that Tracy and I were in some sort of relationship. I ordered Tracy a lemonade and tried to calm her down. She took a sip of the drink and then vomited over Jack's and my feet.

Tracy apologised drunkenly and Jack and I went to the toilet to wash. While we were in the bathroom I explained the Tracy situation to Jack. I told him how Tracy had knocked on my door and how I had not let her in, I also said that I wasn't sure if should get myself caught up in somebody else's situation and asked him for advice.

Jack didn't mix his words. "Do something about it, but be careful, you may have to confront Mick."

Tracy was holding court when Jack and I returned. A group of local men followed Tracy around like buzzards—she had money so it was easy to guess who supplied the drinks, if not the laughs.

A couple of the staff were on the floor cleaning Tracy's spew, so I bent down and gave one of them a tip and asked him to call me a taxi. I finished my drink then, waiting for a lull in Tracy's conversation, I walked over and grabbed Tracy by the hand and dragged her outside. The buzzards tried to follow but I warned them off.

Once we were outside I pulled Tracy around to face me. "You're going home," I said.

She tried to pull away but tripped in a pothole and nearly fell over. I held her up and she tried to hug me. "Come on," she said, "we can go get a drink."

I fended Tracy off. "You're not going anywhere," I said, "I'm sending you home." She looked at me and laughed then tried to walk back into the bar but I kept hold of her. She got as far as her arm could reach then came to an abrupt halt, she pulled against my grip but I held her tight. "You're not going back in there."

Tracy pulled on her arm, she pointed at the bar. "Leave me alone, I just want to go inside," she slurred over her shoulder. "I want to see my friends."

I kept hold of Tracy's arm. "Tracy, they're not your friends, you should go home. I've ordered you a taxi."

She flapped her free arm in the air, the local boys waved at her and I could see Jack behind them keeping an eye on things.

Tracy again tried to pull away, I didn't let her and she rounded on me. "Just fuck off and leave me alone," she said. "I want to finish my drink."

I took a step forward and looked Tracy in the eyes. She struggled to focus. "Tracy, you need to go home, the taxi will be here in a moment."

Tracy nodded. "Yup," she said, then tried to walk away.

I put an arm about Tracy's waist and led her across the road, away from the bar and the local boys. She stumbled with me. "Where are you taking me?"

I propped Tracy against a wall. "I'm sending you home, Tracy. I will pay for the taxi, but you need to go." She slid down the wall and I caught her, I hefted her back up. "You have to stand, mate."

Tracy pushed me away, "I can stand."

I let go of her and she wobbled back against the wall, so I stepped to her side and placed a hand around her arm to steady her. She tried to brush my hand away. "Fuck off," she said, "I'm not going home." She giggled and changed tack. "I will go to your home," she said. "Take me to your house."

I ignored her, lit two cigarettes and passed one to her. Tracy took a drag then threw the smoke over her shoulder. "I know where you live, you live over there," she said and pointed. Her arm swung around in a wide arc. "Just over there."

She couldn't keep her arm up and it flopped to her side. "Somewhere," she said and laughed. "Take me there. Take me to your fucking house."

"Tracy, I'm sending you home. We can talk tomorrow."

She tried to slap me but I pulled away. "I'm not going home," she said, "I will go home with you, but ..." Tracy laughed put her hand over her mouth to cover it.

I tried to keep my voice stern. "Listen to me, Tracy, you can't do this to yourself." I thought I sounded like a dad and I felt like an idiot, wishing I hadn't become involved.

She put a hand on my chest and tried to shove me but I didn't move. "What would you know about it?" she slurred.

"I know you're making a fool of yourself," I said cruelly, then I placed a hand lightly on her shoulder "Tracy, just go home, mate. Sleep it off."

She tried to slap my hand away. "I'm going out," she spat. I could see she was getting angry.

"Listen to me," I said, "I just cleaned your spew of my feet, I'm already sick of this shit. You're going home."

The taxi pulled up beside us. Tracy tried to pull away to the side but I stopped her and she spun back and tried to hug me, I spun with Tracy and danced her onto the back seat of the cab. She flopped onto the seat and I tucked her legs inside. "Tell the driver where you live and do it now, Tracy."

She mumbled out her address, then placed her hands on her eyes and wiped at her tears, smudging her makeup even further. Her face was a mess. "I don't want to see Mick," she sobbed, and I felt sorry for her.

I stuck my head into the car, made sure the driver knew where Tracy lived, then turned to her. "Tracy, I'm going out tonight and if I see you around town I promise I will do the same thing. I promise I will drag you into a taxi by the hair if I have to." I felt like a bully.

Tracy smiled, laughed, then cried harder, black eyeliner tears streamed down her face. "You wouldn't," she said.

I returned the smile and shook my head. "I am not fucking joking. If I see you, I will grab you by the hair and drag you kicking and screaming into the closest cab."

Her smile disappeared and she looked at me wide-eyed. "OK," she whispered, "I'll go home."

I felt even worse. I had meant the threat as a joke, I have never hurt a woman in my life and never intend to, but Tracy seemed to take me seriously.

I decided to let it lie. Bali was a dangerous place for a drunk and lonely woman and I was worried for her safety. I pulled myself out of the car and slammed the door. I opened the taxi's front passenger door and sat next to the driver and asked for his name and put it into my phone.

Tracy murmured something and I looked into the back

to check on her. She seemed half asleep, I hoped she would be alright. I turned back to the driver and took Rp100,000 out of my wallet. It was more than triple the fare. I held up the note so the driver could see it. "This is my friend. Get her home and take her nowhere else. I don't care if she asks you to drop her off at a club, you make sure she gets home and you make sure she goes inside." The driver nodded.

I placed the money in the driver's hand. "This is yours. I will call my friend in fifteen minutes and if she is not at home I'll make trouble for you."

I got out of the car and watched the taxi take off down the street, then went back into to the bar and noticed Tracy's lackeys had left. There was no point hanging around once the cash cow had gone.

Jack sat at the bar waiting. "Are you OK?" he asked.

"Yeah, fine," I said, and took a long swig of beer. "I'll visit Mick tomorrow."

That was the last time I saw Tracy in Bali.

That night I decided I would do something about Mick, but I wasn't sure what. The next day fate supplied the answer.

I was sitting in a bar having a quiet beer when one of Mick's friends rode by. I yelled at him to stop, he did and I called him inside. He walked into the bar and I offered him a beer. He declined and ordered a Coke, and I asked him what was going on with Tracy.

Duncan took a sip of his drink. "Yeah I know, mate, she's become a unit. I'm worried about her also. I had a word with Mick and he says he doesn't give a toss, says it's none of his concern what she gets up too, says she's on her own now."

To me this sounded like a cop out. "Can't you talk to him again, mate? She's going to get herself in trouble. She's been knocking at my door asking for help. She fucking threw up on me the other night"

Duncan shook his head, nursed his Coke, "Yeah, I know mate. She asked me and the lads for help also."

I lit a smoke and offered one to Duncan. He declined and I could tell he was uncomfortable as we had never got along. "And so, what did you do?" I asked.

Duncan frowned, rubbed at his temple. "I've tried mate, I promise, and I'm not the only one. I like the girl as well. A few of us got together the other night and we put it to him ... we told Mick he should do something, but he just doesn't care."

I didn't buy it, Tracy was a long way from home and her ex-boyfriend and her closest mates had abandoned her. Nobody seemed to give much of a shit, especially Mick. As far I was concerned the English crew had made it easy for him to wipe his hands of the situation.

Tracy had then gone out on a limb and asked an acquaintance for help and I'd also ignored her. I felt ashamed of myself. "What if I talk to Mick?" I asked.

Duncan sat back in his chair crossed his arms. "I don't see it. A whole bunch of us were on him the other night. He doesn't want anything to do with her. No offence, but I don't see him listening to you if he wouldn't listen to us."

I shrugged, "Yeah well maybe I should give it a try. Tracy has always done the right thing by me."

I picked up my beer and swallowed it down. "Do you know where he is?" I asked.

Duncan stood up from the table, "Yeah, he's in the restaurant. I'll take you if you want."

I called for my bill. "I'd appreciate that," I said. I thought I might need the back up.

I fixed my bill, paid for Duncan's Coke, then jumped on the back of his bike and we took the short ride to Mick's place.

Mick was behind the counter when we arrived, the restaurant was not overly crowded. Mick greeted us suspiciously. Duncan and I were not great friends and I'm sure he sensed that something was up.

I walked over to the counter. "Mick, can we have a word in private?"

Mick was normally easy going and accessible. "I'm busy. I'll talk to you later," he said.

He carried on with his work, ignoring me and I stood at the counter feeling foolish. "Mick," I said, "it's pretty important that I speak with you, if can you just give me a moment. I don't mind waiting until things quieten down." I looked around the small restaurant, there were three or four customers—it wasn't exactly flat out.

Mick didn't bother to reply.

I wasn't about to back away because he couldn't be bothered. "Mick, if you won't talk with me in private, I'll say what I have to say here."

Mick slammed whatever he was holding down. "Go ahead," he shot, and then walked over to his stove and turned his back on me. "I don't give a shit, say what you want then fuck off."

This surprised me. I had seen Mick deal with drunks and trouble-makers and I had never seen him loose his temper. I'd asked him to have a chat and he'd blown up. "Hey, mate, I'm not a big fan of your tone," I said. "I just wanted to have a talk and I offered to do it in private."

"Fuck," Mick screamed, he threw the spoon he was cooking with towards the sink. "What the fuck do you want to say?"

I turned around. The punters in the restaurant stared at me and I decided I wouldn't go easy on Mick's privacy. "I want to talk to you about Tracy. She's a mess and she's in danger of getting herself in trouble."

Mick turned and charged the counter. He leaned towards me shoving his face inches from mine. "Tell someone who gives a shit," he screamed, then pointed outside. "And get the fuck out of my restaurant!"

I lost my temper. I hadn't expected to be thrown out and I stood my ground. "Do something about it, you fucking coward!" I screamed back.

Mick didn't move. He tried to stare me down.

I looked into his eyes. "If you ever tell me to fuck off again, you and I will finish it in the street," I whispered.

Mick climbed further up the counter that separated us, our faces were close enough to touch. "What the fuck has this got to do with you anyway?" he yelled into my face.

I didn't like the way Mick was acting and I can be a hothead. "I'll tell what the fuck it's got to do with me. Your fucking ex-girlfriend is banging on my door at three in the morning."

I could see this affected Mick. I saw his mind click as he wondered why Tracy would knock on my door at that time of night.

Mick backed off. "She knocked on your door?" He climbed down from his counter. "Why was she knocking on your door?"

"You tell me," I shouted at full volume. "I didn't ask to be involved in your shit but she has involved me. You tell me why she is knocking on my door." I levelled a finger at him, "I never had sex with the girl."

Mick edged back. He calmed down a little and I could sense he was afraid that I would do something. "I didn't know," he said weakly, "what did she say?"

I was still angry despite Mick's retreat. I felt he needed a kick up the arse if he was ever going to help Tracy. I punched the counter hard enough to make him jump. "She asked me for help. Do something about your fucking mess, Mick. You made it, clean it the fuck up!"

I started to walk out of the restaurant but stopped at the door and turned and pointed at Mick. "Put Tracy on a plane and send her home or I will get further involved." I left the threat hanging, smashing the door with the palm of my hand as I walked out.

Mick is not a big guy and later I was not proud of how I'd threatened him but I do believe the end justified the means.

I didn't see Mick for a while and when I did run into him in a restaurant he came up to me. He didn't mince his words. "I brought Tracy a ticket and sent her back to England," he said and walked away.

Mick and I would associate after the incident but it was never mentioned. He is not a bad person but it was a bad situation. Bali breaks people and it broke Tracy. She needed to get out and she needed help to do it.

To give Mick his due, he is the same restaurant owner who later gave a sixty-year-old guy a job after his life savings were stolen.

A Soft Touch

When my mates come to Bali on holiday it's generally to drink copious amounts of alcohol and pick up working girls. For the most part they know where to get drunk; the hookers, on the other hand, are considered my domain.

I work and have to get up in the morning so generally I take these guys out, show them how to approach a girl then split. I'm shy with women but this is business so I find these transactions easy. I then leave my friends to their own devices.

On one occasion I took this a little further and I took a girl to the airport to meet a mate off his plane. I'd already paid her and asked her to act as if my friend was her long-lost lover returning to Bali. I wanted her to put on a show and embarrass my friend. It was a bit of a laugh and my friend was most appreciative.

Travis is an old mate and good friend, he came to Bali to say hello and get up to as much mischief as possible. He also let me know that he wanted to meet a girl. It was Travis' first time in Bali, so I was happy to help.

By coincidence, Travis' brother, Vic, was also in Bali. The night they arrived, Travis, Vic and I decided to hit Kuta.

In Bali it is possible to purchase ephedrine—this is a medication that is often broken down to be turned into methamphetamine, or speed. With effects similar to speed, a lot of young tourists gobble ephedrine like candy. Personally I don't like it and I steer clear of the stuff, but it is easy to get and as far as I know it's legal.

Travis asked me if I knew where he could get some—he wanted his first night in Bali to be one to remember.

I knew of a small chemist that sold just about anything, a Rugby player from Australia had told me about the place. He would make monthly trips to Bali to purchase steroids then take them home and flog them to his mates. I figured the chemist would sell something as simple as ephedrine. I jumped on my motorbike and rode to the chemist, it wasn't far and the lady behind the counter didn't blink an eyelid when I asked for the drug.

I organised two cylinders of about ten tablets each for Travis and his brother.

When I gave the boys the pills I told them that three tablets would be enough to get them going. I said they shouldn't take more as I was uncertain of the effects. I also told them to be discrete as I wasn't 100% sure of the drug's legality.

Travis has never been one for half measures, he gets caught up in the moment and becomes greedy, so within half an hour of being out in Kuta he had finished his cylinder and he wanted to head back to the store for more. I pointed him in the right direction, organised to catch up with him later and left him to find his own amusement.

I was aware that he would feel sick the next morning but I knew better than to try and stop him. I did however forget about the other side effect of ephedrine.

When Travis returned we had a couple of drinks at the

Espresso Bar. The Espresso has a live band that allows patrons to jam with them and Travis is an ex-lead singer who can really belt out a tune. He got up on stage and enjoyed reliving his youth.

Working girls are everywhere in Bali if you know where to look, and there are one or two bars they congregate in when it's early ... and getting them early is sometimes a good idea as these girls have a high turnover rate. Take a working girl home late at night and there is a high chance you'll be traipsing along recently explored tracks.

I would suggest to anyone who takes home a working girl that they offer them a shower at the hotel before proceedings begin. The girl won't mind and she will appreciate the opportunity to shower with hot water—a lot of girls live in cheap rooms that have no water heaters. The girl would appreciate it more if the man showered as well; my experience of Indonesian girls is that they are very clean and they expect their sexual partners to practise the same level of cleanliness.

Condoms are also a must and it is smart to carry your own supply. Working girls will sometimes buy cheap to save money and these tend to break halfway through the encounter. It is worth noting that, depending on which official report you read, the HIV infection rate among sex workers in Bali is estimated to be somewhere between 25 and 50%.

Travis, Vic and I went to Paddies on Legian Street. To my mind, this is the easiest place to pick up a girl. One side of the bar is for tourists, the other is for men who are looking. If a punter wanders in and leans against the bar, sooner or later a girl will saunter up and ask if he would like to spend some time with her.

A little trick is to never set a price in the bar. Too often, guys blurt out, "I'll give you a million for a short time." That's stupid. Whatever you say the girl will hold you to. A better way is to be nice to the girl. If she is working, and interested, she will prompt the encounter—then talk price in the room. It is far more civilised and you have also cut out the competition.

When we entered Paddies, Travis asked me to organise a girl for Vic and him. I didn't mind helping, a lot of guys are shy their first time. It also allowed me to pick girls that I didn't think would cause problems. I organised a girl for Travis and his brother, and I may have organised one for myself but I'm not entirely sure. The three of us left Paddies and went to our respective hotels. I didn't see the boys until the next morning but at the time they seemed pleased with my choices.

The next day when I caught up with Vic he raved about how beautiful his girl was and how great the sex was. When Travis turned up, Vic and I had just ordered breakfast and we were stuffing our faces, but we could tell right away he wasn't happy. I was concerned that the girl I had chosen had done something wrong and I enquired about Travis' night. "How did you go?" I asked.

Travis sat down at our table. "Fucked," he said, and ordered a beer. It was nine in the morning so I knew his night probably hadn't gone as planned.

I looked at my watch. "It's pretty early mate you sure you don't want some breakfast first?"

Travis grabbed his stomach. "Na," he said. "Those fucking pills. I couldn't eat anything."

I smiled. I knew what an ephedrine hangover was like and was glad I hadn't got involved. I shoved a load of scrambled eggs in my mouth. "What happened? Was there something wrong with the girl?"

Travis shook his head, "Na, she was alright. I just couldn't get it up. I tried everything, she sucked it, rubbed it, nothing ... waste of money."

This was in the days before Viagra and Cialis had hit the streets of Bali. Nowadays it's everywhere and the old guys utilise the stuff like you wouldn't believe. I feel sorry for the poor working girls, in a matter of months Viagra increased their workload tenfold.

I felt bad for Travis. His first night in Bali had turned into a fizzler so I tried to cheer him up.

"Must have been the ephedrine," I said. "I wouldn't worry, there are plenty of girls out there. I'll take you out again and set something up."

Travis looked depressed. That probably also had something to do with the ephedrine—the hangover can be lethal. "Na, it's bad," he told us. "I couldn't get it up with that girl, so I took her back and got two more girls. I took them home and still couldn't get it up. I had them naked in my bed and everything. Fucking ephedrine shit, you should have warned me."

"How many did you take?"

Travis thought for a moment, then dismissed the idea of using his brain so early. He rubbed at his temple to ease the exertion. "Fuck, I don't know, fifteen or something."

I had told him to take three. "Fuck off Travis, you fucking idiot. I'm not responsible for your greediness."

He nodded his head and held up a hand to concede my point. "Yeah, I know, but it gets worse," he said. "When I couldn't get it up with those two, I took them back. Then went to a different place and I got four more."

Vic and I gave each other a look. We knew Travis was greedy but he'd taken it to a different level. Erectile problems or not, four women could be considered excessive. "Four?" I asked. "What the fuck did you do with four of them?"

Travis rubbed at his temple. "Well I couldn't get it up, could I? Fuck, I don't know, I thought four would help. I put them all in the spa together then dived in."

I shook my head, stunned. I couldn't believe what I was hearing. "Did that help?" I asked.

"It worked a little. I had them washing each other and stuff. Fuck all though, I still couldn't have sex and there was no way I would have been able to cum."

I bit my lip to stop myself laughing. "Fuck man," I said, "that's a bit sad."

Travis put his beer down, dropped his head into his hands, then shook it. "I had four sexy women in a spa, they drank my drinks and had the time of their lives, and all I could get was a semi hard-on."

I took the opportunity to glance at Vic. He had a hand over his mouth and was holding back his laughter. "What did the girls do?" he asked. I already knew.

Travis lifted his head from his hands. He peered at Vic and me to see if we were taking the piss, picked up his beer, drank what was left and ordered another. "That was the worst part, they thought it was funny. They spoke in Indonesian and I couldn't understand them. It was fucked. The four girls pointed at me and made jokes. I felt about two inches tall."

The dam burst, I couldn't hide my amusement and erupted in laughter. Vic joined me. "You felt two inches or they felt two inches," he said between fits.

Travis sat at the table, he slumped his shoulders, lowered his head. He looked like the saddest man on earth. He had spent the night being laughed at, and the day didn't look like it would be much better. The jokes had already started.

Get Mad and Get Even

Plenty of Western nutters hang around Bali. I recall hearing one expat postulate that families in Australia must be shipping problem relatives to Bali to get rid of them for brief periods when they have had enough. That sounds about right. The mildly deranged ones get ripped off mercilessly but no real harm comes to them from the locals so it's pretty safe for them to wander the streets alone. For the more psychotic bunch, it's a different story.

There is the watch guy who loves looking at people's phones and watches. He also loves to stare at pretty girls but he is relatively harmless. There is the singing guy, who dresses in army fatigues and wanders around pubs and bars breaking into loud song. He is also harmless but he is very fit and perhaps because of the fatigues he does look dangerous. There is a guy known around town as Harry Butler, who once walked along Poppies One completely naked and recently came into my office and helped himself to a shower. This guy is more of a drunk but he does seem to cause strife wherever he goes.

There is another guy who claims to be incredibly intelligent and richer than Bill Gates but he lives in the cheapest accommodation he can afford. This guy is incredibly obnoxious and he will invite himself to a table of unsuspecting victims then espouse his superior virtues. He can become violent and threatening if questioned or ignored. The Kuta rumour mill has it that he killed himself recently; this is unfortunate as he probably only needed the right medication.

There is the tall guy with long red hair who loves to scream abuse at people and who recently screamed at me for polluting the airways with Wi-Fi bugs—this because I was using a computer at an internet café.

And then there is a guy I call Mad, simply because that's what he is.

Mad has caused me a lot of trouble over the years and recently he came close to having me thrown in jail. Mad came to Bali long before me, he is friends with Ankle and he is dangerous when he is not taking his pills—by his own admission Mad is bipolar. He is six foot one, middle aged but skinny and fit. He dyes his hair blonde and likes to walk around shirtless to show off his stupidly placed and poorly inked tattoos.

I mean no disrespect to the people that suffer from this disease; I'm sure it is dreadful and unfortunate for all involved but it is a disease and can and should be treated.

Unfortunately, someone like Mad, who is trusted to self-medicate, can cause enormous grief for undeserving people and it is perhaps a bit unfair that people who are forced to share an environment with a person experiencing bipolar have to suffer because a relative or doctor does not ensure they take prescribed medication. From the start, Mad has been a handful.

Before I came to live in Bali I was aware of Mad's antics. I'd heard how he got a young Balinese girl pregnant then publicly dumped her. She had then tried to kill the baby by drinking Draino and almost died. I'd heard how he had leapt across a two-storey balcony onto another balcony, then hung by his hands above the road and threatened to kill himself, and how he'd pleaded poor and borrowed money from locals then refused to return it. Apparently Mad also had a habit of attacking people from behind when he felt slighted and Bintang bottles were his weapons of choice—perhaps he learned this trick from his friend Ankle?

Mad's problems with my family started after he purchased an apartment from our company. When everything had been signed over and paid for he employed a real-estate company to manage and rent the room. Our company no longer had any rights to the apartment nor received rental equity from the apartment.

Mad first attacked the manager of the apartment complex. He demanded money in excess of what his room had earned in rental and when it wasn't forthcoming he punched and slapped the manager.

This happened on more than one occasion. The manager was a small man about half Mad's size and he was scared to retaliate. He eventually stopped taking Mad's phone calls and he took to disappearing whenever Mad arrived in Bali.

I was not privy to the books, as this was a separately owned company, but the manager informed me that there was a shortfall between what Mad demanded and what the apartment took in rental. This was a messy situation but it had nothing to do with members of our company or the company itself.

Unfortunately, when Mad could no longer find the owner of the management company he came after us.

At any opportunity Mad would slander members of our company. He would force his way into our office and interrupt business meetings or he would scream abuse and carry on like a lunatic when he came across a member of my family in public. Mad performed these petty acts of terrorism at the most inappropriate of times, and business meetings with potential clients were never fun when he was in town.

No matter how many times it was explained to Mad, he could not fathom that his issues had nothing to do with our company. This had a bad effect on business, but our policy was to ignore him and hope that he went away. Mad didn't.

Mad came to see all the members of our company and all the members of my family as persecutors in some evil fantasy where he was the victim. He has had run-ins with most of my family, and what follows are my personal experiences.

My first confrontation with Mad happened in the Bounty Nightclub. I was having a drink with a friend when I spotted Mad pointing me out to the nightclub security, it is a common belief in Bali that club security can be paid to attack a person so I suspected that Mad may have been attempting to set me up.

Luckily the friend I was drinking with was a large guy and a skilled kick boxer. I knew he would back me up if trouble started. This gave me some comfort and I decided to ignore Mad and enjoy my night out. I also figured that if I did nothing wrong the security would have no excuse to cause me trouble.

Mad spent most of the night standing in the corner watching me. It seemed every time I looked over he was glaring or pointing. Eventually it started to wear a bit thin. Mad has a reputation as a person who attacks from behind and I didn't want to get sucker punched when I walked to the toilet. I decided my best course of action was to confront Mad and ask if there was a problem.

Later I would learn that this is one of Mad's intimidation tactics—to this day he stands across the road from my office and stares, it is pathetic and annoying.

Mad didn't like me approaching; he tensed up when I walked over. I could tell my presence made him uncomfortable. This was strange to me. Although he'd had problems with members of my family and our company, Mad and I had never had any real confrontation.

I walked up to Mad and as I got close I saw him pull a bottle off the table and place it on the seat next to him. "Listen mate, I saw you pointing at me before. Is there something wrong?" I asked.

Mad screwed up his face and levelled a finger at me. "Your brother's company owes me money. I know you're involved."

I was drinking from a Bintang bottle. I lifted the bottle and took a mouthful; I wanted him to notice that I was prepared. "You've been told before mate, your problems have nothing to do with us. We do not collect fees from you and we do not rent out your apartment."

Mad slammed his hand down on the table. He leant forward and glared at me. "You lie like the rest of them. You're all a bunch of liars," he accused.

I knew people had taken the time to explain the situation to Mad in the past and I did not want to ruin my night so I decided to let things be. "Look mate, think what you want. Your apartment has nothing to do with me, OK?"

I made to leave but I kept facing him. I edged sideways through the crowd. I didn't want to turn my back on him. He pulled his bottle from under the table and pointed it at me. "I will get you," he mouthed, as I moved away. I was a tired of Mad's antics. I had never done anything that would have deserved him "getting me"—I wasn't even involved in the company when he made his original deal.

I was worried that he would charge through the crowd with the bottle so I stepped back towards the table. I knew the safest place for me was face to face with him. I placed my bottle on his table and looked him in the eyes. "How are you going to get me?" I asked. "Are you going to use that?" I glanced at the bottle in Mad's hand.

He thought for a second, then relaxed his grip and placed his bottle down. "I don't need that, I have a gun. I will blow your head off," he said, and smiled.

The comment seemed absurd and I laughed. "Fuck off! You don't have a gun."

Mad didn't see the funny side of it and his face contorted into an angry grimace. He stood up and leaned across the table and put his face close to mine. "You think I'm joking? I have a gun and I'm going to put a bullet in your head." He then moved back, placed his hands on his hips and stared at me.

I could see he was serious but I doubted he had a gun. I smiled at him. "You have a gun, do you? Well you know what, you're a fucking idiot." I felt the comment was true enough.

Mad didn't like the idiot part. He flinched at the word,

stretched his long arm out and pointed at my temple. "I will put a bullet right there. I will kill you and watch you die."

I kept my eyes on his in case he did something reckless but I felt like I was dealing with an imbecile. I didn't know if it was possible to get a gun in Bali but if Mad had one, he was probably stupid enough to use it. "If you have a gun and you are going to shoot me, why don't you show me the gun?"

I thought this sounded primary school, something one kid may say to another in the playground, but I didn't know how to react; no one had ever told me they were going to shoot me before. "Put your gun on the table and I will believe you," I challenged him.

He took his arm back, cradled his chin and thought for a moment. The ultimatum seemed to bamboozle him. "I can't show you," he said eventually. "If I bring out the gun, security will take it."

The reply was equally childish. "So you're lying then?" I said, and felt like I was involved in an infantile conversation. "I want some proof or I will not believe you."

Mad shook his head; he seemed frustrated that I couldn't understand his dilemma. "I can't show you because the gun is in my motorbike and my motorbike is downstairs. I can't bring the gun inside because the security will take it," he explained irritably.

I was sure he was bluffing but I told myself to be careful when I left the club. "Alright, I believe you," I said, "now that you have given me this information, why don't you tell me when and where you're going to shoot me?"

Mad missed my sarcasm. His expression became serious, self-righteous. "I'm going to follow you home one night; you won't see me and when you least expect it I will shoot you in the head."

Mad smiled. He appeared fascinated by his words, and he seemed to marvel at their brilliance like a child who has written his first sentence on a blackboard. "I'm going to shoot you in the head," he repeated.

Mad's demeanour unsettled me, he seemed disorientated, not quite there; his obvious insanity set my nerves on edge. I wanted the conversation done with. "You know what you should do?" I asked and waited for him to catch up.

He jerked, gripped the table, and glared at me. "What?" he spat.

"You should walk down to your motorbike, get your gun out and shoot yourself in the head."

Mad gawked at me wide eyed and vague; I'm sure he thought I'd been taking him seriously. He took a moment to digest this, then stuttered, "You ... don't you ... you will ..."

I decided to fill in the gaps for him. "I'm serious mate, you're fucking insane."

Mad didn't like the comment. He tensed up and prepared to react. He pushed his chair back and looked around to see if he was being watched.

I didn't want a confrontation and I remembered Mad had been talking to the security when I'd first arrived. I did the first thing I could think of to defuse the situation. I stepped back and started to dance. Mad seemed flabbergasted. He appeared unsure how he should respond, so he leaned on the table and stared at me in disbelief.

I decided to help him along. I made my hand into the shape of a gun, put it to my head and mimed pulling the trigger while I danced.

Mad gaped at me mystified, he mouthed something that I did not hear then looked around for support. I lowered my arm, placed a hand on my elbow and sighted my pretend weapon. I jerked my hand back and yelled, "Bang, bang!"

Mad looped out and knocked the bottle from his table with a swipe of his hand. He pointed at me and screamed and then kicked over his chair and stormed out of the nightclub. I spent the rest of the night with one eye open in case Mad came back with a gun. He didn't, but from that night on he hated me.

The next time I came into contact with Mad was after he smashed a Bintang bottle over the head of a friend of mine. I wasn't present but apparently they'd been involved in an exchange of words in a local pub just off Poppies One in the heart of Kuta. When my friend asked him to step outside and settle it, he refused and my friend made the mistake of turning his back on Mad.

Mad picked up a bottle and slammed it down on my friends head; he delivered him a hard blow that sent him to the floor and left him with a gash in his head that would require fifteen stitches, then he went in for the kill.

Fortunately another friend happened to be watching and took out Mad with a rugby tackle.

The Good Samaritan in this story is all of five feet tall and he weighs about as much as my laptop. His name is Hamish and it was a brave effort on his part. Mad knew both these guys were friends of mine and the next morning Mad came to see me.

This is typical of Mad. One week he is going to shoot you in the head, the next he is your best friend. I guess this is a classic symptom of bipolar disorder.

"Mal, I need to talk to you," he said when he approached, "what happened last night wasn't my fault."

He crouched in front of me. It was early in the morning and I was having a cigarette outside my office. From where I sat I could see three guys sitting in an alfresco restaurant watching us.

I noticed them because you never know when Mad is setting you up, which may sound paranoid but it is part of Mad's MO. He likes to enlist help from tourists, security or the police; it's a wise thing to keep an eye on your surroundings when dealing with him.

I had no idea what he was talking about as I had not heard from either of my friends. "What happened?" I asked sensing that I was somehow involved but unsure how.

Mad looked around and fidgeted. He was nervous and unsure where to start. "Luke and I had a fight last night. He started it. I didn't mean to hurt him but he was taken to hospital."

I sighed, stubbed out my cigarette and flicked it away. Luke was a harmless guy that didn't cause trouble. "Is Luke OK?" I asked, concerned. One of the guys in the restaurant across the road stood up. He looked in our direction and I lifted my sunglasses to let him know I was watching.

Mad rubbed his face and shuffled his feet. "I don't know," he said, "I left after the fight. But he started it. I thought you should know."

I grunted but I wasn't really listening, I had my eyes on the guy in the restaurant, I didn't like his body language.

Mad turned to see where I was looking. He noticed the guy standing at the table. "Hi," he called over and waved.

"Don't talk to me, you fucking dog!" the guy called back.

I was a shocked. It was not the reaction I expected and I stood up. I didn't like to be seated in Mad's presence anyway, it made me feel vulnerable. "Do you know those guys?" I asked. "I don't think they like you."

Mad ignored the dog comment and turned back to me. "OK, I will let you get back to work. I just wanted to tell you the fight was not my fault."

Mad held out his hand for me to shake.

I refused. "OK, bye," I said.

He walked away and I figured he was worried about the guys in the restaurant. This intrigued me so I crossed the road to talk to them. I introduced myself and asked if I could have a word.

The guy who was standing was a big English lad about twenty-five years old. He had a rugby player's build and a boxer's stance, and he looked like he could handle himself. He invited me to sit down and took his seat. "Do you know that guy? Are you a friend of his?" he asked.

I laughed. "Yeah, not likely," I replied. "I call him Mad. Watch him, he's dangerous."

The rugby player scowled. "He's a dog," he replied. "That cunt smashed a bottle over some geezer's head last night. The geezer wasn't even looking."

I could tell the boys were angry. Luke was English but I'm sure this had little to do with it; they just couldn't believe someone would commit such a cowardly act. "The guy's name is Luke, he's a friend of mine. Was he OK?"

The rugby player relaxed and leaned back in his chair. "He'll be alright but he will have a nasty scar." He bent his head down and ran a finger along his skull to show me where Luke had been hit. "His head was split along here," he said. "One of his mates took him to the hospital."

I unwound a little, I was glad to hear it. I liked Luke and no one deserves to be hit with a bottle. "What happened?" I asked.

The rugby player shrugged and looked over at his mates. One of his friends answered for him. "We didn't see all of it. The geezer, your friend, was sitting at the bar with his back to that dog. He gave him a clout to the back of the head with a bottle. A little Scotsman broke it up, we helped him."

I didn't know Hamish was involved. I'm very protective of Hamish—my whole family is. I felt my temper rise. "Little Scottish guy with grey hair?" I asked. I now understood why Mad had approached me.

The rugby player nodded. "Yeah, little fella, grey hair ... he brought the big Aussie down. Me and me mates stepped in and made sure the Aussie didn't retaliate."

"Thank you for that," I said, "he's also a friend of mine. Is he alright?"

The rugby player laughed. "The little bloke, he's Scottish isn't he? Yeah he's fine. Tough little bugger. The big Aussie didn't know what hit him."

I thanked the rugby player and his friends again. I was glad Hamish wasn't hurt but I was annoyed that Mad had brought his special kind of trouble to bear on friends of mine. I left the English boys to their breakfast and called Luke and Hamish to check on them.

Like a coward, Mad jumped on a plane and flew out of Bali that afternoon.

One of the problems with Mad is you never know when he will try and impose himself into your life. He likes to seek out well-muscled tattooed-up people to tell his sob story to in the hope of garnishing their help. Unfortunately for Mad, the next occasion he tried to rustle up a friend, it was an acquaintance of mine.

Jason was eating breakfast when Mad appeared and sat at his table. Mad went into a monologue on how he had been ripped off by a family of business people; he told Jason that these people were going to be taught a very big lesson. Jason had no idea who Mad was but he guessed that he was talking about my family. He listened patiently to what Mad had to say.

Mad told Jason that he'd procured the services of a hitman who had worked for former president Suharto. Mad said he was going to lure one of the members of the business family around the corner from his office then kidnap him at gunpoint. The person would then be bound and gagged and driven to the outskirts of Bali where he would be executed with a bullet to the head. Mad then told Jason that he planned to bury the executed person in a rice paddy.

Jason was a little astonished at this boast and he explained to me later that Mad had simply sat down at his table and rambled on about this without any prompting on his part. Jason did

however ask who the victim was going to be and was s[...]
when he heard a description of me and my name.

Jason then excused himself and he called me. He repeated the
conversation and warned me not to go to my office. I took his
advice and didn't show up.

Mad turned up at my office at ten that morning. He was
accompanied by a large Westerner and a well-muscled Indonesian.
He asked for my whereabouts and was told that I hadn't arrived
for work, then he got my phone number from one of my business
cards and called me. He did his best to get me to the office. I
declined, but arranged to meet him the next day.

The staff called me when Mad and his villainous entourage
had left. They told me that Mad and his friends had done their
best to frighten them into giving up my address but that they had
refused. The following day I arrived at the office to meet with
Mad accompanied by two Balinese gang members and a paid-off
Bali policeman.

Nick organised this and he also came along. Billy sat in the
restaurant across the road. I wasn't kidnapped and murdered but
I did get to meet the bodyguard and he looked the part. Again
Mad demanded money for his apartment and again we explained
that we had nothing to do with his room.

A month later we had another run in with Mad. Mad put
it around town that he was going to bring a group of Balinese
gangsters down to bash us, then he confronted Nick and me in a
restaurant and tried to intimidate us. Nick told Mad to bring it
on and then he arranged a location and a time. Nick, me, the kick
boxer and three Balinese gang members waited for Mad in a pub

at the designated time. Jason, a former heavyweight boxer, also asked to be in on this. I appreciated his offer but refused, I did not want him to get involved in my mess.

Mad arrived alone, it seemed the people he had paid to bash us had declined to show up. He took one look at us, ran to his motorbike, then roared away and was not seen around Kuta for some time.

He now spends his days planning to get back at my family for some perceived mistreatment or other. He could almost be considered a stalker, he wastes time and money and he causes stress to anyone who has become embroiled in his fantasy world.

Things finally came to a head between Mad and me about a year later.

Mad had arrived in Bali for his usual three-month stint. These occasions usually start with him promising anyone who will listen that he won't cause trouble. Unfortunately he then runs out of pills. On this occasion Mad was up to his usual tricks, bad mouthing my family, borrowing money, picking arguments and getting into fights.

One day, while I sat in a restaurant waiting for Nick and a few friends to show up, Mad appeared and walked over to me. He asked if he could sit down, ignored my refusal and sat down anyway. "Mal, I just want to say that this time I won't cause any trouble."

I continued eating. "Listen mate, I don't want to hear it, better I keep away from you and you keep away from me."

He ignored me and proceeded to tell me his problems. "My mother is eighty-nine and dying." "I have no money." "I lost my credit card." "My dog died last year." "My boat sunk." "I went to jail in Thailand." Mad talks in monologue, his stories are at best boring and perhaps it is laziness on my part but I have no wish to repeat them. I have heard them too many times and they are always the same.

Mad believes these things are my family's fault. I have no idea how we killed his dog or made his mother sick or sunk his boat, but somehow my family is responsible. I listened politely and waited for him to finish his conversation. Mad finally finished his rant then got up from the table; he thanked me for listening and walked away.

Fifteen minutes later he returned, sat down and, despite my protests, went through the list again. He did this four times.

Eventually I was joined at the restaurant by Nick, Hamish and their wives and a business associate and friend, Dave. We had arranged a get-together because Nick was ill and due to fly back to Australia for a major operation. The meeting was supposed to be part business, part pleasure.

Everything was going well until Mad re-appeared and asked to join us.

Nick promptly declined. He told Mad that we were involved in a business meeting and that we would like to be left alone. Mad took no notice. He inched closer to the table and proceeded to repeat his hard-luck story. Nick and I looked at each other. "He's been doing it all day," I said.

Nick has had to put up with Mad the longest, and like all of us he has had enough of his antics. "Yeah, he's probably not taking his pills," he replied.

Nick interrupted Mad's blabber. "Hey mate, I asked you nicely the first time. We are having a meeting and we don't want you to join us, so if you wouldn't mind, go away and tell somebody else your problems."

Mad erupted in a frenzy. He pointed at Nick and screamed. "You fucking owe me money. None of this would have happened if it wasn't for you. You're to blame, your fucking family is to blame. You're a bunch of fucking criminals, you're the fucking Mafia."

Nick stood up; he was with his wife and he is very protective. "You're living in the past mate, let it go and leave before you get yourself in trouble."

Mad stepped closer and rounded a chair so he stood in front of Nick. "I was happy when Ankle stabbed you in the throat, I wish he'd fucking killed you!" he screamed. Those of us sitting at the table choked in disbelief at the last comment.

Nick turned at the sound. "It's OK," he said reassuringly. I stood up and walked to Nick's side.

Nick turned back to face Mad and smiled. "Run out of pills have you Mad? You know you're insane. We can all see it, why don't you go and get some help?" Mad didn't take the opening; he pressed forward and twisted his features into a scowl. "I will kill you and your fucking family," he screamed.

Nick is defensive of those he loves; threatening to kill his family was a big mistake. "Go away, boy, leave now!" he said.

Mad underestimated the threat. He flexed away from the table and thrust out his chest. "Do something then. Come on, I will fuck you over!"

Nick rounded his shoulders. He was about to let loose and I have no doubt he would have destroyed Mad, but he was also ill and he was with his wife. I knew he wouldn't be happy but I decided to intervene, I stepped up and punched Mad hard in the side of the head.

I'd reached the end of my tether. It wasn't the best punch, but it rocked Mad. He stumbled into the street, grabbed at his ear and stared at me dazed. "You're a fucking dog," he screamed.

I laughed. I had nothing to say and waited for him to bring the fight back to me.

Mad checked his ear for blood. "What are you laughing for?" he bellowed. "You king hit me, you dog."

"Yes." I said and laughed louder. I felt good. I released a lot of pent up frustration with that punch.

"You fucking dog," Mad screamed, "you king-hitting dog."

I pointed at Mad. "Does it hurt?" I asked and smirked. I couldn't wait to tell Luke that I'd given Mad a dose of his own medicine. I remembered the apartment manager and how Mad had bullied him. Fuck you, I thought, how does it feel now?

Mad realised he was going to get no joy from me, so he turned to Nick. "You too," he yelled, "you're a fucking dog too, your whole family are dogs."

I took a step forward. Nick reached out a hand and grabbed me. "Let it go for now," he uttered, then told me to sit down. "Let the fuckwit carry on making a fool of himself."

I sat down, turned my chair to face the road and pulled my sunglasses down. I lit a smoke and stared at Mad with a smile on my face.

Nick turned to Mad. "Take a look at yourself, mate. You're insane. We know it and you know it. Go get some help."

Nick sat down and picked up his drink. "Ignore him," he said to everyone at the table.

Mad rose to the bait. He paced up and down and hurled abuse at us. "I have friends," he screamed. "Irish boxers. I'm going to bring them down and give you and your brother a hiding." Mad pulled his phone from his pocket. He called someone, spoke briefly and then shoving the phone away he continued to pace. "There is going to be an old-fashioned brawl," he screamed at Nick and me, "five boxers and you two. When my friends get here there will be blood on the streets."

Nick smiled at Mad, "Bring it on, crazy boy. We'll be waiting."

Mad stood and stared at Nick, he'd tried to intimidate him to no avail. He shook his fist at us both and stormed off to get his boxer friends.

We watched him leave and then huddled around our table. Nick and I told Dave and Hamish that they should go; we said it was our problem and they didn't deserve to become embroiled in a negative situation with Mad.

Hamish and Dave refused and said they would join the fight if the boxers turned up, they said they wouldn't abandon their mates no matter how many showed up.

Nick then asked his wife and Hamish's to leave and they also refused—both women started making phone calls.

Indonesian women are incredibly loyal and dangerously inflexible when it comes to their husbands or family being threatened. Nick's wife organised two rough-looking security guards to come down and sit at a table behind us. Hamish's wife rang her cousins in the police force.

Nick then got up from the table and asked me to keep an eye on things. He crossed the road to where we were getting construction work done on our office. He organised the Indonesian construction workers to join the fight with hammers and shovels if the Irish boxers turned up. He promised them a large bonus for anyone they took out.

Mad was right about one thing, if his boxers did come there was going to be blood on the streets.

Mad turned up half an hour later. With him was a heavy-set bald man whom nobody recognised. This stranger kept his distance, pacing back and forth at the end of the road and making phones calls. Every now and again he gestured or pointed in our direction. He then rode past us on a motorbike a couple of times. He took a good look at us but evidently decided it wasn't worth his while and left after the second pass. Mad watched him go then leapt onto a motorbike and rode past us with a skinny Indonesian on the back. Nick and I smiled at him as he passed. We didn't know if he was going to return, but decided to hold our ground. We remained at the restaurant.

We were soon joined by two Indonesian intel officers. They were very powerful men and cousins of Hamish's wife. The high-ranking police officers sat with the Indonesian women at a table across from us.

We ordered food and drink for the intel officers and the security, and sent *nasi* (rice) and a few Cokes over to the workers, then settled in to wait.

Eventually we were joined by two more police officers. Unfortunately, they had been organised by Mad and had come to arrest me.

The Indonesians then sat down to talk. After a brief discussion, I was called over and informed that Mad had made a statement against me for assault. I was told that I would have to go to the police station and make a statement or I would be arrested. I was also notified that the punishment for assault was six year's jail and a fine.

Nick's wife jumped on her phone and organised a very powerful ally to come to my aid and Hamish's wife assured me that I wouldn't have a problem as long as her cousins were with me. I consider myself very lucky that I have such loyal Indonesian friends.

When I arrived at the police station I was informed that the charge had been upgraded to assault with a weapon causing injury. I found out later that Mad had scratched himself on the neck, enough to draw blood, and that he had told the Polisi I had attacked him while wearing a ring. I do not wear jewellery.

I was in a lot of trouble. I faced a hefty fine and jail time. A lot of people, including Nick, pulled together to get me out of the mess I had landed myself in.

Indonesian police stations are not fun. I have been to a few on unrelated issues. You sit for hours, nobody tells you anything and the Indonesians yell and scream at each other. It's daunting.

Eventually Nick, his wife and I were led into a small room to be interviewed. Nick's wife got herself involved as translator—she is a very shrewd and steadfast woman.

Mad was seated at the desk with an Indonesian police officer and he smirked at us when we entered, he seemed confident and dabbed a tissue at an injury on his neck.

When I first arrived in Indonesia I learnt from Nick that the key to dealing with Indonesian authority is to always be polite. Mad also seemed to know this and he did his best to flatter the police officers dealing with our case. What he didn't count on was Nick sitting next to him.

Nick took every opportunity to goad Mad and get him to show his real personality. This wasn't difficult to do and it was funny to watch. Mad struggled to control himself when Nick poked him verbally, and on more than one occasion he blew up at the police sergeant, which definitely worked in my favour.

The interview went well for me, I had a lot of people watching my back and credit definitely lies with them. For my part I was nervous and I kept my statement short. I denied hitting Mad and claimed I had given him little more than a push. I said I had no idea why he was bleeding and that Mad's red ear had nothing to do with me.

I then went on to tell the police that Mad had threatened my life and the life of my family on more than one occasion. I told them that he was indeed crazy and that the whole thing was a hoax on his part.

During my interview the intel police came into the room and patted me on the shoulder; one even whispered to me that I would be alright, despite the seriousness of the situation and my nervousness. I felt I would be OK. What I didn't know was that Mad had promised to pay money if I was put in jail. It became a sticky situation and only the high profile of my backup saved me. The interview dragged on for an hour before I was told I could leave and that no charges would be brought against me.

After this incident I decided to get out of Bali for a couple of weeks. I wanted some time off work and chose to spend two weeks in Thailand. I was glad that I did. Mad did not give up on me, especially when the whole side of his face, including his ear, turned black.

The Kuta rumour mill churned when I returned and more than one person told me that they had seen Mad lurking around with a gun. This still seemed unlikely as guns are not so easy to come by in Bali but Mad had threatened to kill me on a number of occsions in the past.

When I returned to Bali from Thailand I was glad to hear that Mad had left. Unfortunately, I was soon to learn that he'd arranged a going-away present. Not long after I arrived back I received a letter summoning me to the police station.

Mad had supplied pictures of his injuries and he had somehow reopened the case. I learned later, through Nick's connections, that he'd paid a lot of money to have me thrown in jail. This time I didn't feel comfortable contacting Hamish's wife for protection, but I was lucky enough to have Nick's wife firmly in my corner. A good example of this woman's strength is the admonishment she gave me after I punched Mad.

Nick's wife took me aside and said, "Mal, next time you want to hit someone, tell me and I will pay someone to do it for you." She is not a woman to be messed with.

With Nick's wife's help and a few of my brother's connections

I managed again to get out of the situation, but it did cost money. The money was delivered to the police station in a brown paper bag late at night by the powerful ally that Nick's wife had organised.

I have never asked how much was paid but I was glad it was. I was also glad to have loyal, determined and intelligent people on my side.

To date, after seven years, Mad has still not given up on me. During the writing of this book I received a phone call from another Bali policeman. Mad claimed that I owed him money for somebody that stayed in his room without paying. The absconder was a friend of mine and the bill was not paid, but it had nothing to do with me.

Unfortunately I know Mad's logic. In his mushed-up mind either my family or I are responsible for everything bad that befalls him. I'm sure money will change hands again in an attempt to have me locked up and I'll deal with it when it happens. I do wish the guy would just take his medication.

Mad isn't smart but he is conniving, manipulative and paranoid. He needs help and he needs to be taken off the streets of Bali before he hurts someone or himself.

I should mention that one of the gang members that joined my office in a security role took me aside and volunteered to murder Mad for me. He told me that if I wanted him to kill Mad and get rid of the body, the fee would be thirty million rupiah (about three thousand Australian dollars). He said my only obligation, after payment, was to look after his family should he be caught and sent to jail. I declined this offer. I had no wish to kill anyone,

Mad included. I did however take the offer seriously. This security guard had stabbed two people in the past and he'd spent time in jail for both stabbings.

Spatial Awareness

Bali is known worldwide as a great holiday destination: a fun place to visit and a tropical paradise where millions of tourists come every year for their vacations. One of the most common reasons people give for choosing to spend their holidays in Bali is the people. The stock phrase is: "Balinese are wonderful people, they will do anything for you."

This is true up to a point. Indonesians are delightful people and most of them work extremely hard to make a visitor's stay in Bali a wonderful experience. However, there is also an undercurrent of jealousy and anger that permeates through some of the local Kuta community. I have heard Indonesians scream at Westerners: "This is my country. If you don't like what I do, get out." And I have heard this sentiment on more than one occasion.

A lot of Indonesians, Balinese included, are jealous or fed up and they don't like Westerners. This is the reality. The sooner an expat or tourist learns this, the better off he or she will be. I have read so many columns and letters in local newspapers expounding the fact that a Westerner has been slighted or ripped off by an Indonesian. All of these have an undercurrent of disbelief that an Indonesian could possibly perpetrate a misdeed against a Westerner who spends money in Indonesia.

I believe this is a naïve way to think, there are many Indonesians who are sick of rich Westerners holidaying in their country. They couldn't give a toss about the money and they would prefer to have their island back.

Anyone who has lived in Indonesia for any length of time also knows that Indonesians win most legal battles against foreigners. In my opinion, Indonesian law favours the Indonesian, and Indonesians know this—unfortunately, most Westerners do not.

A frequently seen form of petty extortion employed in Bali against Westerners is for Indonesians to yell and scream in the hope the Westerner will try and make the problem disappear with cash. It is true that when confronted by irate Indonesians, Western tourists tend to panic.

Watch any motorbike accident that involves a Westerner and you will witness Indonesians crawl out of the woodwork. They will accuse and threaten the Westerner until he or she hands over cash, even if the accident was the Indonesian's fault.

Creating altercations with Westerners can be a win-win situation for Indonesians and I have personally been confronted by Indonesians on a number of occasions—in some of these cases I was at fault, in others I was not—but the result of most these exchanges has been to show me the real agenda behind aggressive Indonesian confrontation.

Disagreements between Indonesians and Westerners happen all the time. The simple rule is that no matter what the circumstances, never retaliate or you will come off second best. My first confrontation with an Indonesian was with a lifeguard on Kuta beach.

I had been involved in a running race and as I rounded the flag I reached out and used the pole to turn myself. Although I barely touched it, the lifeguard claimed I had bent his flag and demanded I replace it for a fee of one hundred Australian dollars. I refused and the lifeguard did his best to provoke me into fighting him. I sat and smiled while the lifeguard stood in front of me and called me every name under the sun.

This took place in front of a group of friends and other tourists and it carried on for an hour.

The non-retaliation rule wasn't hard to comply with in this circumstance—no matter what this guy called me and no matter how many times he challenged me, there was no way I was going to fight him. In the end another Indonesian became involved on my behalf and the lifeguard relented, but all in all it was embarrassing and an unnecessary attack and its sole purpose was to extract money.

Another confrontation occurred after I allegedly scratched an Indonesian's car. I was barely moving in gridlocked traffic yet somehow I was supposed to have scratched the car beside me—a pink Suzuki Karimun. I bet that the occupants of the other car were bored and when they saw a Westerner they saw an opportunity to make some money.

Anyway, an Indonesian man got out of the passenger side of the bright pink car next to me and came to my window and accused me of scratching his car. I told the man that I hadn't scratched his car but he didn't accept this and he called me few names before challenging me to a fight.

I did the only thing I could do: I wound up my window and

ignored him.

The Indonesian screamed for five minutes then he gave up and returned to his silly pink car. The company car I drove at the time didn't look much better; it was a Daihatsu Terios that was such a bright shade of blue it could be seen from space.

I thought the incident was over when the irate Indonesian gentleman returned to his car. I sat back to wait out the traffic jam, only to see the man send in his wife.

The lady walked over to the front of Gay Blue—one of many names my hideous car went by—and spat on my windscreen. This wasn't pleasant but I decided to accept it. I thought once she had vented her anger she would go away and I turned on my widescreen wipers to wash away her spit. Unfortunately this seemed to anger the woman further and she went ballistic. She raised her fists and slammed them down on the bonnet of the car. Gay Blue had a shell as thin as paper and the irate woman left two fist-sized dents.

I was horrified so I bravely did the only thing I could think of to help my situation: I pulled my sunglasses down, turned up my stereo and I smiled.

This only incensed the crazy Indonesian woman further and she walked around to my window, screamed and then did her best to punch me through the glass. This didn't work but I thought she may have hurt her hand so I mouthed the word "ouch" then shook my hand sympathetically.

Crazy Indonesian Woman didn't see the funny side of this either and decided to kick her way through my car door. Gay Blue was insured so I did the polite thing and I gave her a round of applause for her effort.

She then decided that dents to only half of Gay Blue would look out of place, so she proceeded to kick every panel on the car. She even put a few dents in Gay Blue's roof.

I had no choice but to sit and let Gay Blue get beaten up by a crazy woman and when the lights changed and the traffic cleared I inched the car forward. I was worried she would fall off the roof but I couldn't sit there all day—I also felt sorry for Gay Blue.

Eventually I reached the traffic lights and with the nutter gone from the roof I zoomed off. I thought this would be the end of the confrontation but of course it wasn't.

The Indonesian lady ran back to her pink car and she and her companion pursued me around Kuta.

The two brightly coloured cars must have resembled two giant M&Ms as they raced around town. This was my first car chase and I knew Kuta well. I drove past all my favourite haunts hoping someone would see me race by with the pink car in hot pursuit.

The couple eventually gave up but sadly Gay Blue was severely dented because a couple of Indonesians saw an opportunity to make some money.

These stories are funny to me and I didn't take what happened too seriously, but sometimes you can find yourself in real danger if you retaliate. It is better to remember that you are being confronted for money and to smile, wave and leave.

The Prostitute Girlfriend

Sanur is the brothel capital of Bali and everyone who lives here knows it. At one stage the company I worked for had an office there and if I was ever asked by an Indonesian where I had spent the day and I replied Sanur, I was met with sly looks and giggles.

The brothels in Sanur litter the back streets like Circle Ks litter Kuta. Turn a corner and you will find one, but while Circle Ks display the "K" logo, Sanur brothels are marked with an "X". Anyone driving through Sanur need only look for the crudely painted symbol on the front walls of the compounds.

Most Sanur brothels are little more than carparks dotted with small rooms where the girls sleep by day and work from at night. As many as half a dozen seedy gangster-type Indonesians can be found hanging around each carpark. During the day one of these guys will wake up a girl for a customer but at night when a car or taxi pulls up the girls will swarm out of their rooms like mosquitoes.

Some Sanur brothels have a small dark café somewhere on the premises—these places are dangerous and should be avoided. There is also a Sanur brothel that employs a window system—in Bali, as in Bangkok, it's called a goldfish bowl. Men enter and look at the girls from behind mirrored glass. A lot of guys like this but I find it dehumanising.

I have never been a big fan of Sanur. Kuta and Seminyak working girls meet their clients in clubs and they have a personal choice as to whether they want to leave with the customer. The working girls in Sanur brothels have little choice and due to the process of obtaining these girls, the brothel system smacks of sexual slavery.

Generally, a brothel owner visits a poor village in the back blocks of Java, they meet a group of girls and entice them to come to Bali with the promise of a job and accommodation. The brothel owner then flies the girls to Bali and they sign a three-month working contract to pay back the money. These girls tell their parents they have found work in a restaurant, or as household staff, and they send all their money home. They have little chance of paying out their contracts unless they work very hard and accept as many clients as possible.

I don't like to be a party to this process and so I don't frequent these places.

This is not the case with all girls working in Sanur, however, and there are girls who re-sign their contracts and refuse to leave even when given the opportunity.

A friend once told me how he met a Sanur working girl and he talked her into coming to live with him. Rob met Nenny and fell head over heels in love. She was about twenty-eight, quiet and comfortable to be around, and Rob said he couldn't get enough of her.

Rob told me that rather than visit Nenny in a brothel night after night he had asked her to give up her life and live with him.

He told her that he would supply all her needs, take care of her family and that he would help her find a proper job. Nenny agreed to Rob's proposal and she left her workplace and her belongings and went to live with him.

On the first day of her new life Rob took Nenny shopping. He bought her a new wardrobe and Rob told me that Nenny put on a fashion show and proudly paraded around in her new things. He said that she seemed incredibly happy and that she cooked a nice meal and the two of them settled in to watch a movie.

Nenny was sitting on the couch in her new pyjamas when there was a knock on the door. Rob answered it and was met by two Indonesian men.

The Indonesians demanded to speak to Nenny and Rob led them into his home. Nenny and the Indonesian men spoke for some time and although Rob speaks fluent Indonesian he couldn't keep up with the conversation as the group spoke in a dialect he had trouble following.

Eventually the discussion stopped and Nenny informed Rob that she was going back to the brothel to continue working.

Rob tried to bargain with the Indonesians. He offered to pay out Nenny's contract on the spot, but the Indonesian men refused. They motioned Nenny to follow and the three of them left.

Nenny didn't take any of the things Rob had bought for her, she left wearing the pyjama's she had on.

When Rob told me his story I inquired how the Indonesians knew his address and he explained that he had taken Nenny out of the brothel on a previous occasion and she had been picked up from his home.

Rob missed Nenny but he left it for a few days before he attempted to speak to her. He did not want to have a run-in with the brothel owner or his henchmen.

One night Rob called Nenny and asked if they could meet. She told him they could meet at the brothel where she worked.

Rob went to the brothel and paid for a room so that he could talk with Nenny in private. She informed Rob that she would be staying at the brothel and that he could wait for her if he chose and that she would come and live with him when she had finished her contract.

Nenny's contract ran for another two months and Rob decided to wait it out, he also paid for her to visit him on occasion. However, when she finished her contract Rob asked her to come home with him, Nenny refused and took another contract. To my knowledge she still works at the brothel.

Rob told me he was incredibly disappointed but he continued to visit Nenny and do his best to convince her to leave the prostitute life—he paid for this privilege.

When Rob told me his story, he invited me to meet Nenny. I was intrigued so I took him up on the offer.

Rob took me to the brothel where Nenny worked and he introduced me to her. My impression was that Nenny was neither pretty nor polite, and she looked as though she would have done well to get out of the business.

Rob had a legitimate love for Nenny and I believe he would have done his best by her, for her part Nenny chose life as a working girl over a life with Rob.

A Lesson from Billy

When I first arrived in Bali, Billy took me to a club where a punk band was playing. There were about twenty or thirty Indonesians sitting politely on the floor in front of the stage watching the band.

Billy said he wanted to show me something. Suddenly, without warning, he jumped onto the dance floor and began slam dancing. The crowd who had been sitting patiently immediately surged forward en masse and surrounded him. It happened so quickly and came as such a shock that I thought the crowd was attacking my brother. I shat myself and ran into the crowd with a beer bottle in my hand.

Billy found me in the crowd. He grabbed me by the arm, looked into my face and smiled to let me know things were OK. Then he dragged me off the dance floor and led me to a quiet area of the bar.

My adrenalin was pumping, I was bewildered and shaking. And I still gripped the large empty bottle of Bintang. I rounded on Billy: "What the fuck was that? I thought they were going to kill you."

Billy smiled and told me to settle down. "That's what I wanted to show you," he said. "Indonesians don't take the initiative. They may threaten, they may yell, but they tend not to make the first move. You can stare them down or you can walk away, but if you move on an Indonesian, they will move on you as a group."

Billy had lived in Bali for three years and I was a newcomer. I have never forgotten the lesson.

I once took the kick boxer to the same bar and showed him the same trick. I wanted him to understand the mob mentality of Indonesians and I thought I could teach him the same way Billy had taught me.

I timed it right and when we arrived a large crowd sat watching a band, patiently waiting for somebody to start the dancing. I did as Billy had shown me: I walked to the centre of the dance floor and did my best slam dance.

The Indonesians rushed me as they had rushed Billy on the previous occasion. As one, the large crowd stampeded towards the dance floor.

Unfortunately, this time a European tourist made the mistake of charging in with the Indonesians.

The kick boxer was pumped full of adrenalin from earlier events, he didn't realise what was going on and he thought I was being attacked. He rushed into the crowd.

The kick boxer grabbed the European in a Muay Thai headlock, twisted him around so that he stood behind him, and forced him down onto his arse. When I arrived he was about to bring an elbow crashing down over the European's forehead and onto the bridge of his nose.

I grabbed the kick boxer from behind and dragged him away from the bewildered Westerner, who fled from the club. I watched him leave and when I thought he was safe, I let the kick boxer go.

I asked him why he'd assaulted the European.

The kick boxer looked at me slightly dazed. "I thought you were being attacked," he said. "I didn't want to hit an Indonesian, there were too many so I took down the only white face I could see." The kick boxer shook his head confused. "Did I do something wrong? I thought that's what you said: don't hit the locals."

I smiled at the kick boxer, placed an arm about his shoulder and laughed. At least he knew better than to punch an Indonesian, I thought.

I have never showed that trick to anyone again.

Violence in the Street

Not only do the Indonesians fight each other but Westerners and expats do as well. For the tourists it is more alcohol fuelled, as they pour down arak-filled mixed drinks like lolly water; for the expats it is the frustration of living in a place like Indonesia.

The first fight I had in Bali was in the late afternoon and I was in a depressed state. I had been living in Bali for about two years and I missed my children immensely. My ex-partner was blocking my calls to them and I hadn't been able to contact them for some time.

I had been through a very nasty break-up and, as far as I was concerned, I had no choice but to get as far away from my ex-wife as possible. This meant leaving my children and living in a foreign country ... I struggled with this for a long time.

On this particular afternoon a mate and I went to have a few beers after work. I wasn't in the best frame of mind and a couple of beers with a good friend seemed like the perfect remedy. We had a few beers in our usual haunts and then decided to find a new bar to drink in. I had noticed a new bar some days before and it being some distance from our normal hangouts, we decided to give it a try.

When we entered the tavern it was pretty much empty of

patrons, just one person sat leaning on the bar talking to the barman.

Dave and I were a little disappointed but we had come a long way and didn't want to turn around and head back. Besides, the bar had a pool table and we decided we should have a few beers and see if any people arrived. Dave went to order at the bar while I began to set up the pool table for a game.

I was just about to break when the guy seated at the bar called over to me: "Hey, mate, that's my pool table." Being Australian, I recognised the twang, and the rule.

I looked over and recognised the guy as an expat who had called an associate of mine out of a bar for a fight a few months earlier. The associate had refused to fight and the bloke at the bar had levelled all kinds of abuse at him. He had called him a weakling and a coward, amongst other things.

I had watched the argument but had not become involved. It wasn't my quarrel, but the incident had irked me. I felt the expat at the bar had taken things too far.

It also bothered me that a person who was by himself had claimed the pool table—where I come from it takes two people to play pool. Who did you win it from, I thought, but did not voice.

I broke the pack and then called the guy over. "If you want to play, we'll play," I said, then handed him the pool cue. I wasn't in mood to have the guy inflict himself into my company so I was abrupt.

The guy took the cue then introduced himself as Brett. He then said, "I only play for beer."

In Australia, pub pool rules dictate that the person who owns the table has the right to name the stakes. I knew this but wasn't really happy about it. I probably should have checked before I started to play, but I still felt as though I had been tricked. Brett was getting me offside very fast. "Yeah, whatever," I said and went over to where Dave now sat with our beers.

Brett was a good pool player. He beat me hands down so I went to the bar and bought him a beer.

Brett accepted his beer then looked me up and down. "Next time you walk into a bar, check no one is using the table before you set up," he said.

I shrugged and let the comment roll off me. I had no wish to get into an argument over pool etiquette. "Yeah, no worries mate," I said.

As I returned to my table I heard Brett laugh behind me, "Easiest fucking beer I've ever won," he boasted loudly.

I shook my head and smiled at Dave. "Your game," I said.

Dave has lived in Bali a long time, and if you live in Bali long enough you learn to meet idiots on a regular basis.

Dave and Brett played the next game and Brett won another beer. I watched but did my best not to draw attention to myself. I didn't like Brett's attitude and I didn't want to have anything to do with him.

Brett then looked over to where I sat and challenged me to another game. "Hey loser," he said, "you want to play me again?"

I grimaced at the comment, raised a hand and dismissed Brett. "Yeah, not really into it mate," I said, "it's your table, you can do what you want with it."

Brett laughed, "I know it's my table mate, and I will do

whatever I want with it." He carried his pool cue over to where I sat. He pulled out a chair, leant on the back-rest and looked down at me. "You're afraid you can't beat me."

I took a good look at Brett. He was about my height and weight and of a similar age. "Look mate, I didn't really come here to play pool, I'm happy just to sit here and have a beer." I turned away hoping that that would be the end of the conversation.

Brett swung the cue over and tapped the table leg to get my attention. When I turned to look at him, he said: "That's just bullshit. You're afraid, aren't you?

I clenched my jaw and gritted my teeth. "Yeah, well, it is what it is," I said, and turned away again.

Brett stopped tapping, got up from the chair and mocked me. "I'm just happy to have won a beer from you," he said, and laughed. "Shit, don't you even want to win your beer back?"

I rose to the jibe, I couldn't help myself. I didn't like it that Brett was mocking me. "OK, you want to play? Let's play." I growled. I stood up from the table and reached for the pool cue. "Let me guess, you want to play for a beer, right?"

Brett pulled the cue away. "That's the first rule," he said, "the second rule is the loser sets up the table."

I snatched the cue out of Brett's hand. "This is the last game," I said. I walked to the table and started setting up for a game.

Brett joined me. He checked my set and moved the triangle a millimetre. "This will be the last game because you will lose," he said. I pulled the triangle off the table, placed it on the overhead light, and went round to break the pack.

As I was about to shoot, Brett pulled the triangle off the light with his cue. "It doesn't go there," he spat, and gave a smug look. I ignored him, broke the pack and walked back to my table.

I did my best to beat him but I lost. Halfway through the game I sunk the white and the black at the same time.

I looked for Brett and saw that he was at the bar talking to a couple of Indonesians. "Hey, mate, you won," I called over.

I pulled out my wallet and placed enough cash for a beer on the pool table. "Your money is here," I said loud enough for him to hear, and went back to my seat.

Brett left the bar and stormed over to the pool table. "What the fuck is this?" he said, looking down at the notes.

I was just about to have a drink so I put my glass down and turned around. "There's enough for a beer," I said.

Brett picked the notes up and waved them at me. "You're fucking joking, right?"

I wasn't sure what Brett was getting at. "You won, and there is enough money there to buy a beer. What's the problem?"

Brett laughed and threw the notes down on the pool table. "Get to the bar and buy me a beer," he demanded.

Brett's demand annoyed me. I took a deep breath and managed to remain calm. "The money is on the table, mate, take it and buy yourself a beer."

Brett scooped up the money and shoved it in his pocket. "You're a fucking sore loser mate," he said.

I turned my back on him and raised my eyebrows at Dave. "This fucking guy," I whispered.

Dave smiled. "Fuck him, he's an idiot, just ignore him." He tapped the base of my beer glass. "Drink up."

I picked up the beer and took a mouthful, "Yeah, you're right, he's just another Bali idiot."

"You want a game, there's no competition here!" Brett called loudly to one of his Indonesian mates. I knew the comment was aimed at me but I ignored it and eventually heard the crack of pool balls and guessed a game had started.

Brett played a few games but every now and again he would call over to me with comments like "did you see that shot?" or "bet you couldn't make a shot like that".

I wasn't watching and I had my back to Brett, but the remarks were started to wear thin. I didn't understand why he would want to push me unless he wanted to fight.

I'm not the biggest guy but I do have a shaved head, a bad goatee and a number of tattoos. I wouldn't flippantly pick a fight with a guy who looked like me unless I had something up my sleeve.

Brett was about my size but he seemed too confident. There was something about his attitude that didn't add up and it made me wary. I was about to learn what that something was.

Brett finished a game with the Indonesian and began setting up the table. "You want a game, loser? Come on, I'll go easy on you," he called over.

It was enough to push me over the edge. I turned around to face Brett, "Hey, mate, I don't want to play and if you don't mind, I'm trying to have a conversation with my friend."

Brett laughed. He leaned back on the pool table, mimicked what I had just said. "Oh, I'm having a conversation with my friend," he made a limp-wristed action, "what are you, fucking gay?" He laughed and turned back to his set.

I was seething, I'd done my best to be polite and I had put up with Brett's behaviour for a long time. I looked over at Dave, "This might kick off, watch my back." I slid my chair back and stood up. "That's fucking it," I whispered.

I stormed towards the table. Brett had his back to me and didn't realise I was coming. I noticed Brett's pool queue was leaning close to where he was setting up so I made a beeline for the cue and wrenched it off the table. I didn't intend to use it as a weapon, I just didn't want Brett to go for it.

Brett turned to face me. He took a step back but smiled, he must have seen the anger on my face. "You going play me or hit me with that?" he sneered. I didn't answer. I stood facing Brett with the pool cue in my hand. I wanted to size him up. I wanted to look into his eyes and gauge his strength.

Brett must have taken my silence for fear. He regained his confidence, smiled and swaggered towards me. He stopped when we stood face to face. "Yeah, because you can't play. You're a fucking loser," he said, his voice thick and mocking.

I smiled at Brett and lifted the cue. I let it roll back and forth in my hand and I waited for him to look down. "You can't beat me with this," I said.

Brett watched the cue as it rolled back and forth. He sniggered, stepped back and sized me up. "You won't beat me in pool," he said.

I looked into Brett's eyes, "I'm not talking about pool."

Brett looked confused and gestured towards the cue. "What do you mean?" he asked.

I continued to roll the cue in my hand. "I will give you the cue and you can have one free hit," I said.

Brett still didn't get my meaning. "And then?" he asked.

I smiled. "And then I will take you outside and beat the crap out of you."

Brett looked around anxiously. He fidgeted as he tried to work out if I was serious. "You want me to hit you with a pool cue?"

I threw the cue onto the table. "Pick it up loser."

Brett looked incensed. "What?" he grumbled angrily "What did you call me?"

I grinned. "I called you a loser," I replied, "now pick up the cue and hit me. You get one shot."

Brett stood and stared I could see him try and work out if I was being sincere, "You want me to hit you?" he muttered.

I pointed at the cue. "Go on, mate, it's a good offer. I'd take it if I was you."

Brett remained motionless. He looked perplexed, his eyes flickered, he looked towards the queue and I saw his hand flex. "You will let me hit you?" he asked.

I stared at Brett. "Yep, and then it's my turn." I pointed at the cue. "Pick it up."

Brett thought about it for a moment then he took a step back and raised his hands. "I'm not going to hit you with a pool cue," he said and shook his head.

I took a step forward. I was happy I had called Brett's bluff but I didn't intend to let him off lightly. "You have pushed me all afternoon mate but it seems you are the loser and the coward."

Brett moved around and put the table between us. "I don't want any trouble," he said.

I turned to Dave. "Do me a favour mate and get the bill. I'll fix you up later." I turned back to Brett. "Last chance. I'm going to leave, do you want to use the cue or not?" Brett shook his head. I could see he was angry but also nervous.

I was glad the confrontation was over. "You should be more careful who you call a loser, mate," I said, and then walked out of the bar and went and sat on my motorbike. Dave walked out of the bar a moment later, jumped on the back of the bike, and we rode away.

Fate is a funny thing. When Dave jumped on the back of the bike I had ample time to get out of the area. I was also pointed in the direction I wanted to go, but for some reason I turned the bike and went the wrong way towards a dead end. I had no intention of doing this. I had said my piece and I wanted to get as far away from Brett as possible. I can only put the mistake down to an overload of adrenalin.

I travelled about fifty metres up the road and came to the dead end. I turned the bike around and drove back towards the pub. I planned to ride past and head to a bar where I felt welcome. What happened next surprised me as much as any experience I've had while living in Bali.

When I approached the pub, Brett stepped out onto the road with four Indonesians, two either side of him. I suddenly realised why he had been so confident. He had been setting me up. Brett and his new-found friends fanned out across the road and blocked my path.

I may have been able to drive around them but I had Dave on the back and I doubted I would get through without being kicked from the bike. Dave and I were heavily outnumbered.

Dave is a staunch guy but he is not a fighter. I couldn't put much stock in him and he didn't deserve to get hurt for something I had got myself involved in. I did the only thing I could do: I parked the bike about ten metres back from Brett and his posse.

I stepped off the bike, passed my helmet to Dave and told him not to get involved. I then marched towards Brett and his henchmen.

As I walked towards the group, Brett said something to his bodyguards and they all laughed. I didn't care, the time for words was over. I was trapped and ready to fight my way out. I kicked off my thongs and focused on Brett.

The Indonesians at Brett's side were the danger. I knew if they got involved I stood no chance. I had to scare them off and I had to use Brett to do it. I planned to hurt Brett as hard and as fast as possible, and I planned to be brutal.

Brett and I came together with a punch—my punch connected, his did not. I felt a crack as my fist exploded into Brett's face. Brett swung wide and his punch grazed my chin.

Brett stumbled backwards and I followed. I placed my left hand behind Brett's head and I drove my right fist into his face.

Brett toppled over and I rode him down, his head striking the concrete. I rose up and slammed my right fist into Brett's nose and I was rewarded with a crunch when it broke. I showed no mercy. I lifted myself up and hammered another punch into Brett's mouth. Blood spurted all over me and my hand shattered with the impact.

As Brett's head lolled to the side, I heard Dave behind me shout, "Stay back! Stay back!" I looked up and saw the four Indonesians looming over me. I kept my eyes on the Indonesians as I checked my hand—it was broken and useless. I got to my knees and smashed my elbow into Brett's face. Brett exhaled sharply then moaned and went quiet. I knew he was finished and I stood up to face the Indonesians.

The fight had only lasted a few seconds, not long enough for the Indonesians to react, but my hand was broken and I was surrounded by Brett's henchmen. They fanned out and faced me. I spread my arms wide and looked them in the eye. "Motherfuckers!" I screamed, and waited for them to move.

The Indonesians took a step back and I stepped forward. I tried to make a fist and screeching pain shot up my forearm. I looked down at Brett and saw him fighting for consciousness. I had done what I had needed to do. I had taken him out of the fight.

Brett was finished but I was far from done. I looked at the Indonesians and could see they were nervous. "Come on, you fuckers," I shrieked, but no one moved.

I noticed one of the Indonesians was standing on my flip flops so I strode towards him yelling, "Are you trying to steal my fucking shoes?" The Indonesian stared at me wide eyed and then he stepped away from my thongs.

The Indonesians saw a crazy man—it was what I wanted them to see. I was scared they would attack me and I knew I could no longer fight. My broken hand pulsated and I needed them to back off.

I noticed movement from the corner of my eye, turned slightly and saw Brett stand. I watched as he stumbled backwards trying to hold onto a wall. He then slid to the ground like a battered drunk.

The Indonesians watched Brett fall and they turned as one and fled.

I stood my ground and watched the Indonesians run but then I heard somebody scream "call the police!" and I knew it was time for me leave.

I ran to my motorbike. Dave stood next to it with his mouth open. He gaped at me, stunned.

"Are you alright?" I asked. Dave didn't answer, he looked horrified. Shocked, he stared at my chest.

I followed Dave's eyes and glanced down at my shirt. It was covered in blood. I jumped onto the bike and screamed at Dave to get on the back. He hesitated for a moment and then joined me. I revved the bike—my hand hurt on the throttle but I ignored it—then raced the engine and sped away.

I rode to an out-of-the-way pub, gave Dave some money and asked him to go and buy me a singlet, then I went to the toilet to wash up. I looked in the mirror and saw my face and arms were covered in blood. I cleaned myself up then ripped the un-bloodied part of my shirt into strips and bandaged my broken hand. I dumped the rest of the material. When Dave returned with a singlet, I put it on and we went to the bar for a beer.

Only when we sat down to drink did Dave finally manage to speak. He looked at me amazed and shook his head. "That was the most violent thing I have ever witnessed," he said.

I felt embarrassed. I didn't know what to say. I tried to close my hand and it hurt. I felt I had got off lightly and I could imagine Brett hurt a lot more than I did.

"Yeah, well," I replied, "I'm not real proud of myself right now." I felt awful. Brett had made an error, he'd picked the wrong guy at the wrong time. I was upset about being away from my children and all I wanted was to be left alone so I could talk to a friend.

I'm not a violent man but I know how to get there. I grew up in a rough part of town with three brothers and everyone wanted to fight us. When we weren't fighting each other we were defending ourselves.

Brett couldn't have known this. He just happened to choose the wrong person. This is not a boast—what I'm trying to say is that Bali is like that, you never know who you are going to meet or what their history or circumstances are.

Maybe I should have been more patient with Brett. But he had blocked my path and threatened me five on one. Had Brett faced me alone I would have knocked him down and been done with it. Unfortunately he left me with little choice and he paid the price.

Bali is like a frontier town in an old Western movie. It attracts the scum of the earth and the truth is you never know who will have the fastest or biggest gun.

I got lucky that day and I think it was because I was so scared. I have no doubt that had I not acted so fast and in such brutal fashion that it would have been me left on the side of the road in a heap.

This happened quite a few years ago. I don't know how badly I hurt Brett but I have not seen him in Bali since.

Thumbs up

For Hamish's buck's party—his bachelor party or stag night for non-Antipodeans—I wanted to hire sexy dancers because strip shows are illegal in Indonesia.

The Indonesian Government is very strict on pornography and recently an anti-pornography bill was passed that threatened Bali's very existence as a holiday island: under the new law bikinis are supposed to be outlawed.

This anti-porn bill has also led to the internet-download speed being reduced to prevent porn from being downloaded, and resulted in the publisher of *Playboy Indonesia* being sent to jail, even though the magazine contained no nudity.

A funny footnote to this is that one of the proponents of this law, and an important Member of Parliament, was recently photographed looking at porn on his tablet during a parliamentary sitting. I found this incredibly funny in an it-can-only-happen-in-Indonesia kind of way.

During my time in Bali two strip clubs opened and both places lasted about six months before they were shut down resulting in the foreign owners of both establishments losing a lot of money. I do not know the circumstances regarding the closure of the first place, but the second strip club was shut down because it became overran by Indonesian gangs.

One practice employed by foreigners owning nightclubs in Bali is to impose cover charges for Indonesians to enter a club—something that is often condemned as being racist. The reasons club owners give for this practice are a) Indonesians do not drink much, b) foreigners do not like to go to clubs and be surrounded by Indonesian men, and c) Indonesian gangs take over the clubs, extort the staff and start trouble with the foreign clientele. The latter is apparently what happened to the second strip club.

The owner thought he had done the right thing by paying the right people, unfortunately he neglected to charge a door fee and within months a gang set up shop in his club. The owner was soon forced out and the gang tried to run the club with little success.

Indonesia's solution to its lack of strip clubs is sexy dancers—this phenomenon came to Bali about five years ago and now sexy dancers can be found in the more popular and upmarket clubs.

The lack of strippers in Bali can be a real headache for anybody asked to organise a buck's party. I have been asked to organise two in the past—for Hamish's party, I arranged sexy dancers, but, unfortunately, the buck passed out an hour before they arrived.

For the other buck's party, I tried something a little different. It was an impromptu affair. The day started out like any other and finished with a wild party. It's funny how many Bali days are like this, you just don't know what will happen by day's end. On this occasion, there were four of us sitting in a pub when Chris blurted out that he was heading to Java the following day to meet his girlfriend's family before tying the knot the day after that. He gave me very little time to work with.

Everyone looked at me for a solution. "You're the guy that does the buck's nights, what's the plan?" they asked. I have no idea why or how I got the job, it just seemed to be gifted to me like an unwanted present.

I had hired a group of sexy dancers for Hamish's buck's night, so I guess this explained some of it, but although they had done a good job and everyone seemed to enjoy the night, they were expensive and they had to be booked a week in advance. They also cost four hundred dollars for three fifteen-minute shows, cheap by Australian standards but expensive for Bali.

Unfortunately, I had no plan and I'd been given a couple of hours to work with—also afternoon romps in Bali generally turn into a disaster. I picked up my phone and turned it over in my hand, thinking. Suddenly the answer struck me—it was literally right before my eyes.

I was involved in a legitimate business in Bali and I didn't feel it was appropriate for me to always hang around in prostitute pick-up joints. One of the tactics I employed to manage this problem was to always request the phone number of any girl I took home—over time I had managed to fill my phone with numbers of working girls. I told Chris that I would see what I could do.

I left the bar, went around the corner for a bit of privacy and then sent a text message to every hooker in my phone:

"*500.000. Three hours work. No sex, txt back*"

My phone rang almost instantly. Ira was on the line. "Hello darling, how are you?" she asked.

Ira was a girl I would occasionally call when I needed a bit of company. Twenty-six, smart and stunningly beautiful, she was always available for me as we got along well, but she was very expensive and she would never stay the night.

Ira preferred to do short-time visits, and when things were finished she would race back to the club so she could turn over a few more tricks.

She was open and honest about this. She said she'd almost finished paying off a house in her village of Banyuwangi and as soon the house was paid for she intended to quit work and marry a Javanese boy she'd been dating. She was a vibrant and happy working girl with a plan, and she had become a monthly treat for me—with the price she charged it was generally on payday.

I asked Ira if she was busy and if she had three like-minded friends. "You and your friends will not have to have sex, just a swim and a party, and I will buy the drinks," I said.

There were reasons for the no-sex request: I didn't want anyone to get too excited and try to have sex in the pool with one of the girls. I liked where I lived and pool sex in the afternoon would surely have seen me evicted. And I didn't want one of my sleazy mates to sneak a girl into my room, as I'm not a big fan of other people having sex in my bed. Also, I wanted the party to be fun—I didn't want the expectation of sex to spoil the mood. Or perhaps I was simply jealous—I didn't want to share Ira with one of my dodgy mates.

Ira said she was interested, but she sounded a little unsure. "No sex? Why you want girl but not want sex?" she asked me suspiciously.

I tried to reassure Ira. "It's just a party," I explained, "my friend get married and we want girl to help celebration."

Ira interrupted me, "But you pay girl for sex, then you just want for party? I never see do like this before."

I could see Ira's point. I had offered enough money for a normal client–working girl arrangement. I also knew it was pointless to argue and try to explain over the phone. I figured I would explain it to her in person and give the guys the rules.

"Ira, just tell your friends that they must bring bikini, OK? Tell them they will not have to have sex, we will just be having a swim party. If friend not have bikini, I will buy one for them."

Ira paused. I didn't know if she was struggling with the no-sex concept or the fact that she needed to find three friends with bikinis. Eventually she came back on the line. "OK darling, I come. I bring my friend live same *kost* me. I will looking other girl, is OK?"

I was happy I had at least two girls to join the party. "Yes, is good Ira, call me back when you find other girl, ya?"

I went back to the bar and told Chris and the other friends that I had organised something and their bill for the afternoon's entertainment would be five hundred thousand each. "Oh, and you may have to buy a few pairs of bikinis," I added.

"Bikinis," one of them, Mitch, piped up. "What have you organised?"

I smiled, and felt proud that I had at least been able to arrange something. I also wanted to set the rules right off the bat. "I may have four girls for a pool party at my hotel. They're working girls but they won't be available for sex, just drinks, giggles and a few swimming lessons."

The quip about swimming lessons seemed to get everyone over the line, they all seemed happy with the arrangements.

There were a few arguments over who would have to go to the shop and buy the bikinis but it kept the boys busy while I waited for Ira's return phone call.

Ira called me back a moment later. "Hello darling," she said. "I have three friends and we want to go swim in pool, no sex and you give five hundred, ya?"

I laughed. Ira was smart and a very good businesswoman. It was one of the things I liked about her. She wanted confirmation of the price and the contract before she committed. "Yes sweetheart, five hundred and no sex."

Ira giggled excitedly, "I and my friend will come and swim in pool afternoon ya, I meet front gate your hotel in one hours, OK darling?"

I smiled at the lads; I could see they were hanging onto every word. "OK darling, I will meet you there, and bring bikini ya." I hung up the phone and gave the boys a thumbs up.

Back then I rented a one-bedroom apartment with a kitchen and large bathroom for four thousand Australian dollars a year. The compound I lived in was built in the early Nineties and boasted thirty hotel rooms set in beautiful tropical gardens. Situated on the Denpasar side of Legian Street it was far out enough to be quiet but close enough to town to make the nightclub scene accessible. By far the room's best feature, however, was its proximity to the hotel's large, and private, swimming pool.

The swimming pool had a pool bar that was usually staffed

by a young Balinese. I didn't know what sort of reaction I would get rolling up at three in the afternoon with three horny blokes and four prostitutes, but I had made the arrangements and I had little choice but to move ahead.

I needn't have worried for the pool was empty when we arrived. I spoke to the pool boy and told him to stock up the bar with Bintang beer and Mix Max.

The boys jumped into the pool but I stayed dry, I wanted to ensure that the security would not extort the girls and so I had to escort them into the hotel complex.

The guys had been swimming in the pool for about thirty minutes when Ira called. "I'm at your front gate with my friends," she said. I didn't need to be told twice, I went to pick up the entertainment.

The girls were waiting for me but they were surrounded by the hotel security. Ira looked typically stunning; she wore a soft yellow see-through summer dress and she her long, silky hair cascaded over one shoulder.

We walked a small distance away from the security and then Ira introduced me to her friends. "Darling, this is Sinta, this is Putra and this is Ita."

I shook the girls hands as I was introduced but when I came to Ita I stopped, stunned.

Ita was dressed similarly to Ira, she was about the same age and shape and she had a matching hairstyle. The two looked so alike that they could have been sisters. I kept hold of Ita's hand and turned to Ira. "Darling, you the same," I said. "Are you from the same family?"

Ira laughed; she reached down and took my hand from Ita's. "Yes," she said, "Ita is my cousin."

I turned to take another look at Ita, my mouth fell open and I turned back to Ira. "Blood cousin?" I asked amazed. They looked like the same person.

Ira dropped my hand then she went over and placed an arm about Ita's shoulder. Standing together it was hard to spot the difference. "Of course darling, Ita comes from the same village as me, my mother and her mother sisters," Ira pointed to her face then Ita's, "see we look the same, stupid."

This was the good news and I figured the boys would be very happy; the bad news was the other two girls.

Whereas Ira and Ita were stunningly beautiful, Putra and Sinta looked like they had been picked up off the street. They were skinny and they had bad skin, they looked worn and beaten and were simply not in the same league.

I took Ira aside and asked why the other two girls weren't pretty. "I'm sorry darling," she replied, "is afternoon, ya, all girl sleep afternoon, only my cousin and Ira awake. I must find girl extra by looking, you want many girl and is difficult me to find."

Ira said this as though it explained everything and I was a fool for asking but I had a sneaking suspicion that Ira and her cousin had organised cheaper girls so they could split the majority of the booty. This was confirmed moments later when Ira stipulated that I pay her at the end of the day so that she could pay the girls.

I didn't mind. I felt Ira was only trying to make a buck and she had done a wonderful job organising and bringing the girls in the first place. Besides, I'm not exactly Brad Pitt and who was I to be fussy. "Yes darling, I will only give money to you," I replied.

I pulled Ira back to her friends and explained that we were having a buck's party. "I want you to have a good time and be nice to Chris. No sex, just have fun." I then asked the girls if they had bikinis. Ira looked at the girls and they giggled. "Darling, we not bring."

I dropped my head into my hands and shook it. "Oh great," I said, expecting that I would be spending the next hour shopping for bikinis.

Ira laughed and put an arm about my shoulder. "Don't worry darling, this is not a problem. We Indonesian girl, we don't need bikini to go swimming." The girls giggled and nodded in agreement.

I found myself caught between wanting the girls to take their clothes off and wanting to be allowed to continue living at my hotel. "Ira not too much ya, is day time, maybe there is some families around."

Ira pecked me on the cheek, "Stupid man always worried. Come on, take us to the pool. We want to go swimming."

The girls jumped about excitedly when Ira mentioned the pool. I knew I had no choice but to take them, but I was still concerned. It was daylight and four naked girls in the hotel swimming pool presented a bit of a problem.

Ira knew the location of the pool and the girls streaked off ahead of me. As they sniggered and laughed, I wondered what I had got myself into.

When we arrived at the pool the boys playfully invited them in. The girls weren't shy and they whipped off dresses and pulled down jeans.

This was the moment I'd dreaded. I was sure the girls would strip down to nothing and I was worried about the pool boy's reaction. I needn't have worried, the girls went as far as bras and knickers.

The girls stood about half-dressed and the boys in the pool went quiet. They stared, mouths ajar. The scenery was exquisite, much better than sexy dancers.

Ira came to my side and put an arm about my waist. I rested a hand on her beautiful thigh. "Darling ,can we go in the water now?" she asked and jumped up and down.

I let my hand travel up Ira's warm, smooth, lithe body. "Of course, baby," I said. Ira didn't need to be told twice. She howled something at her friends in Indonesian and then she unceremoniously dumped herself in the water.

Ira's friends followed suit. The boys in the pool swarmed over and the pool boy laughed and clapped—the party had commenced.

The buck's party started out pretty tame. The girls were happy to be in a swimming pool and we were happy to sit in the pool and have a few drinks and a laugh. A couple of the girls attempted to swim and I was pleased to see they were semi capable ... having said that, there were a lot of eager teachers available.

Ira and Ita received the most attention but the other two seemed content. It was a comfortable environment, there were plenty of drinks and the music was loud and rocking. Things only became wilder when Ira and Ita decided they wanted to dance. Ira swam to my side and asked if it was OK. I said it was fine by me. It was one of the things I liked about Ira, she was a complete business woman and very professional with her job. She felt it was important to entertain Chris in the style of a buck's party and didn't need prompting.

Ira and Ita then climbed onto the pool bar and started grinding to the music. The girls had spent a lot of time in nightclubs and they could move exceptionally well—they seemed to enjoy themselves and they danced as well as any practised sexy dancers. Ira and Ita put on a great show and the other girls soon joined them. The whole group seemed to be having the time of their lives and they played up to the slack-jawed men in the pool.

The pool boy had the best view and he clapped and laughed along with the girls and the music. It was a great show and it improved dramatically when Chris called out, "Ira, take off your bra!" Ever obliging, and without hesitation, Ira turned Ita around and undid her bra. She threw it over her shoulder into the pool, then turned for Ita to do the same for her—the other girls followed suit.

The pool boy had four semi-naked women gyrating on his bar. The girls pretended to kiss and cuddle as they danced. I could tell the pool boy had never witnessed anything like it before. He stopped clapping and just stared, his expression was one of unmasked bliss. The girls must have noticed the pool boy for they whispered amongst themselves then turned away from us and gave the pool boy his own private show. His face split into a big bright Balinese smile, and I could see it was the happiest moment of his life.

As the girls danced a song for the pool boy, we were presented with four cute wiggling bums, then each girl took a turn to climb into the bar then as a group they surrounded the pool boy and kissed and a cuddled him. I was sure I heard a small groan of pleasure emit from the bar.

The girls climbed out of the bar and ran back around to the pool. They were all jiggling boobs and clinging wet knickers—even I was impressed by what I had organised.

When the girls re-joined us in the pool, the pool boy caught my attention. He placed his hands together, bowed his head and said, "Thank you."

I had to smile. "No, thank you," I replied.

Indonesian girls can be very territorial. I was only a customer but Ira wouldn't let Ita near me, which was fine as to achieve this Ira had to spend most of her time at my side. This did wonders for my ego but I was sure the others understood. I had known Ira a long time and it was natural that she would want to spend time with me but I did my best to share and I sent Ira over to the other guys on more than one occasion.

Problems began when Chris became territorial over Ita.

We'd all had a laugh, a drink and a good swim. It was harmless fun and there had been no funny business until Chris corralled Ita and dragged her to the other side of the pool. We all knew what Chris was up to and despite it being his buck's party we felt it was a little unfair. We had all understood from the start that the girls were there to entertain, not be roped and groped.

Ira swam over to me and complained, "Darling, why your friend take Ita over there?" Ira pointed to the other side of the pool. I looked over and saw that Chris had Ita in a corner, his arms were either side of her and with limited swimming skill she had little chance of escape.

The scene annoyed me. "He stupid man, Ira. I sorry he not good behaviour," I said as my anger slowly rose. At the time Chris was a good friend, but I had gone out on a limb for him and I felt he was taking the piss out of me, the girls and the other blokes in the pool.

"Ita tell me before, darling, she not like where he want put hand. Stop him darling," she asked. This may sound strange as the girls were working girls, but even working girls deserve a bit of decorum and Ita wanted to be with the group and have fun.

Also a contract had been agreed on and the girls had held up their side of the bargain. Ira and Ita had a right to be annoyed as far as I was concerned so I swam over to Chris, lifted his arm and set Ita free. Ita moved away from Chris but held onto the edge of the pool; I could see she was afraid to tackle the deep end by herself.

"What you doing, mate?" I asked Chris. "You know what was decided. The girls are here to entertain, they're not here so you can get you're jollies on the other side of the pool."

Chris smiled at me drunkenly. "Yeah, but it's my buck's party," he said.

Chris was about to ruin what had so far been a fun day; I put an elbow outside the pool and held myself up. "I don't care mate, we're all here to have fun. You don't get the pick of the litter."

I could see Chris wasn't happy at being interrupted. "What's it got to do with you?" he snarled.

I didn't bother to argue. "It happens again and I'll send the girls home," I said, and hoped my threat would settle him down.

I turned away from Chris and took Ita by the hand. I swam her to the other side of the pool, passed one hand to Mitch and the other to Tony, and then swam back to Ira. "Go and swim with your friend, darling," I said. I pointed at Chris. "It will help keep him away." Ira thanked me, kissed me on the cheek, and joined the crowd on the other side of the pool.

I had hoped the crowd would keep Chris away but it didn't work. Chris bade his time and as soon as the opportunity arose he grabbed Ita again and dragged her away.

I'd had enough. I wanted Chris to have fun but he was spoiling it for everybody, and I knew Ira well enough to know that if she got her back up she would cancel the afternoon and take her friends home.

I was about to swim back over to Chris and react angrily when one of the other guys in the pool stopped me. "I have a better plan," said Mitch, "watch this."

Mitch called the two skinny girls over, sat them down next to me on the steps then spoke to them in fluent Indonesian that I could not pick up.

The two older girls nodded their understanding, and swam towards Chris. They managed to corner him and Ita slipped away.

Mitch pulled Ita into the water next to him; they leant on the wall and stared at Chris. I slipped into the water and swam up to Mitch and Ita. I was curious. "What did you say to them?" I asked, pointing at the skinny girls.

Mitch took a sip of his beer. "Just watch," he said and we all turned to look at Chris.

Chris was at the other end of the pool. He leant against the wall and I could see he was trying to get around the two skinny girls but they held hands and blocked him in. Also, Chris looked like he was too drunk to escape.

Suddenly Chris yelped. He turned to face one of the skinny girls. "What are you doing?" he squawked. The other girl edged around behind Chris. I saw her drop a hand beneath the water and Chris yelped again. "What the fuck!" he shrieked, and turned to the second girl. He then yelped again. "Shit!" he exclaimed and turned back.

"Stop it," Chris bawled and he pushed himself off the wall and tried to swim away, the two girls following in hot pursuit. I had to laugh. Chris was drunk and not a great swimmer, the girls caught him easily.

One of the girls grabbed him by the foot, she pulled him closer, edged around and grabbed his shoulders. The second girl moved behind Chris and climbed between his legs. The girls lowered their hands simultaneously and Chris emitted a long and painful shriek.

Chris called to us for help but we ignored his pleas, we were in hysterics. He pulled himself closer to the pool wall, backed himself against it and held up a hand to try and fend off the skinny girls.

The girls took a place either side of Chris, laughed and shoved their hands under the water. Chris hiccupped out of the pool and squealed like a pig.

Ita and I were bawling with laugher, and I looked over and saw Ira and Tony cackling. Only Mitch knew what was going on, he had an all-knowing smile on his face. "What the fuck did you say to them?" I asked him through fits.

Mitch tightened his grip about Ita's shoulders. "I told them that it was Chris's buck's party and Western tradition is that girls are supposed to stick their thumbs up the arse of the man getting married."

I laughed, it was fucking brilliant.

Mitch laughed with me. "Yeah well, the punishment sort of fits the crime," he said, and then turned to Ita. "Darling, why don't you and Ira go and help your friends." Ita giggled, turned to Ira and spoke in Indonesian. The two girls made their way over to join in on Chris's anal rape.

Mitch, Tony and I grabbed a beer and settled in to watch the show. The girls were relentless and they were very good hunters. We watched for the next fifteen minutes as Chris had digits rammed into his colon by four Indonesian hookers.

Eventually Chris learned his lesson, sulked his way out of the pool and went home to join his future wife. I would have liked to be a fly on the wall when he tried to explain his red and swollen anus.

Ira, Ita and the two older girls stayed well past their allotted time. I would like to believe they had a nice time swimming and relaxing, but eventually the two older girls swam up and asked if they could leave. I said it was OK and thanked them. I told the girls that I would pay Ira and that they could collect from her and they agreed.

Mitch and Tony also took their leave. We'd had a few laughs and everyone understood the arrangement.

This left me alone with Ira and Ita and I took the girls to my room so they could shower and get dressed.

Once they were inside and Ita had gone to use my shower, Ira made me an offer that knocked my socks off. Ever the business-minded girl, she asked if I liked her cousin. I turned away from Ira and tried to hide the fact that I was about to lie. "I love you too much, I only look at you baby," I said.

Ira slapped me gently and smiled. "You're lying. I see how you looked at her in the pool, you like Ita," she said.

I placed an arm about Ira's shoulder, smiled and did my best to look innocent. "I'm not lie sweetheart, and I only look once darling. Accident," I said.

Ira pushed my arm away. She dropped her towel then stood up and faced me in her wet knickers, "Would you like to have us both?" she asked. "We could stay longer if you want?"

I was stunned, my jaw dropped. "Will I have to pay?" I said and my voice cracked, exposing my eagerness.

Ira looked at me like I was the most stupid man on earth. "Will I have to pay?" she repeated and laughed.

I felt like an idiot and blushed, but I still didn't get the whole joke. OK there wasn't going to be a freebie, I thought. Little did I realise that Ira was setting me up for a bigger fall.

Ira called out to her cousin in the bathroom. She spoke in Indonesian but I could guess what was being said. I heard Ita laugh as well. Ita came out of the bathroom wearing a towel, the girls had a brief giggle-pitted conversation in Indonesian and I sat in my own home embarrassed. When I'd tired of being the butt of the joke, I put a stop to it. "How much?" I asked.

Ira and Ita looked at each other and laughed all the harder.

"We not go together you stupid man," Ira said, between fits of laughter. "*Goblok*, we are cousins! That is yuck, we cannot do!"

I felt like an inch tall.

I rode the girls home on my motorbike and all the way they laughed at the stupid white man. When we arrived, Ira raced inside to go to the toilet and Ita offered me her phone number. I'm ashamed to say that I took it.

Mike Tyson with a Machete

Wyan came to us by way of his uncle, Rap. Rap had been head of our security for some time, he was Balinese and a fit-looking and well-muscled man in his late thirties. He was genial and polite and he was always found to be honest. Rap commanded a lot of respect and he was given a lot of responsibility. When we needed money collected, we called Rap; when someone in the company was threatened, we called Rap; when there was a dispute amongst the workers, we sent in Rap.

Rap was a scary-looking dude but the first thing you noticed about him when you met him was the large bat that he had tattooed across his forehead. He was also high up in one of the Laskar Bali gangs and he had connections with the Balinese police. Once, when he thought the situation warranted it, Rap turned up to a meeting between a Western client and Nick carrying a pistol. He told Nick that he had borrowed the gun from a Polisi friend— Nick told him to keep it hidden in his belt. On another occasion a client who had reneged on his bill threatened Rap with his police contacts. Rap shoved the man backwards and then beat his chest. "I am the fucking police," he screamed into the bill dodger's face. Needless to say the debt was quickly fixed up.

Rap worked for our company for four years, he was well

paid and when he needed help he felt comfortable seeking and receiving it from Nick.

When Rap's child broke his leg in a motorbike accident Nick and the company paid all his son's medical bills and when Rap's nephew was released from prison and he needed a job Nick supplied it even though he knew Wyan had been sent to prison for stabbing his two previous bosses.

Wyan came to work for the company as second in charge of security—there were only two security guards but Wyan liked the title and no one liked to argue with him. Wyan was a large man, heavily tattooed and very well-muscled; he had a striking resemblance to Mike Tyson in looks, body size and personality.

Wyan had the presence of a wild animal. He looked, acted, and made you feel that he was a predator, but he did it with unsophisticated innocence. He was a bull of a man with a quick temper and a childlike control over it. He was a good friend to have when he was on your side but he was fucking scary when the tables turned.

It was a normal day at the office when Nick stopped Dave and me to tell us that Wyan had turned. This was expected. It happened often, even with the most trusted of our employees.

Wyan had worked for us for about three years and although there had been a few minor indiscretions he was liked and trusted, there was also a healthy dose of fear in that mix.

Our company was involved in a building project in Bali and there was often a lot of pilfering that went on during any development. Wyan had been put in as head of security at the current project to stop the pilfering.

Nick explained to us that Wyan had approached him some time earlier because he wanted to supply bricks for the development. Wyan had a friend and he had made a deal; the problem was that Wyan's bricks were more expensive than our regular suppliers. Nick had no problem using Wyan's contacts but it was foolish to pay a higher price for the same product. He made this clear to Wyan, stating that if he could get his price down to at least level with our suppliers, the company would use his bricks.

Wyan was only trying to make a buck, he had a family to support and, as we would learn later, a habit, but Wyan was liked and loyal enough that his proposal was listened to. Wyan tried to get the price down but he couldn't, so he began using his power and his status to disrupt the work site. He began by stopping our supplier's trucks from entering the building site. This was a major problem because any construction site has time requirements and on our site penalties applied. Wyan was head of security and he had the building site staff cowered, so at first we had no idea that he was sending our trucks away. Because of our penalty clauses there were a few times that we had to use Wyan's bricks. Eventually Nick's brother-in-law, Made, who also worked for our company, discovered what Wyan was up to and he informed Nick. (Made is Balinese and is married to Nick's wife's sister.) Nick was left with no choice but to summon Wyan to a meeting at the office.

When Wyan entered the office he appeared agitated. He kept a hand behind his back and he shifted from side to side, his eyes flicking back and forth. Nick approached Wyan and said they needed to talk.

Wyan made to walk towards Nick's private office but Nick stopped him. "It's OK," he said, "we can talk here."

Nick seemed on edge and it surprised me that he didn't address Wyan in his office. Despite what had been going on, Nick liked Wyan and he wouldn't have wanted to berate him in front of us.

When I asked Nick about this later he said that he sensed something was wrong as soon as Wyan entered. He didn't like the way he kept his hand behind his back, he said it felt like Wyan was hiding something. Nick couldn't have known that Wyan had brought a knife.

I sensed there might be a problem, but it was Nick, and not Wyan, that alerted me. Nick just didn't seem himself. He was boss of the company and in that role I had seen him confront people, including Wyan and Rap, many times. Wyan was a scary guy but that would not have affected Nick, who was confident in his role and not a person easily intimidated.

When Nick spoke to Wyan he kept his voice calm and polite. This was very unlike my brother and to me the personalities and actions didn't match the occasion. I kept close to Nick. I didn't over step my authority but I made sure I stood behind his shoulder.

Nick and Wyan stood in the centre of the office and Nick tried to explain the problem. "Wyan, I can't have you stopping my trucks. I've told you, if the price comes down to what we are already receiving, I will use your product, but until that happens I have to go with the cheaper bricks."

Something about Wyan seemed strange. I thought this was because he was in trouble—I realised too late it was because he was on meth.

Wyan rocked from side to side and kept one hand behind his back. "Boss," he replied, "I need money for my family. I want you to use my supplier. I have worked for you a long time, when are you going to look after me?"

Nick controlled himself but it was very much out of character. He kept his eyes on Wyan's face. "I know you have problems Wyan, but I do too. It's bad business to buy expensive."

Wyan stopped swaying and hunched his shoulders. "Do you say my product is not good?" he asked aggressively.

Nick shook his head and took a step back. He put distance between himself and Wyan. "I'm not saying that. I'm saying your product is expensive. It would be bad business for me to buy off you."

Wyan moved his head from side to side cracking his bull neck and he took a step forward. "Your business is bad, you do bad business," he accused Nick.

Nick didn't rise to the bait. There was tension in his voice, but he spoke coolly. "Wyan, we can work on this," he raised a placating hand, "for the moment it is bad business that you are stopping my trucks. This is what we need to talk about."

Wyan baulked at the accusation. The tension rose and his eyes darted around the room. "Why do you speak like this to me? I am second head of security."

Nick again stepped back from Wyan and he pushed me back with him. Nick kept Wyan at arm's reach but he was still in the danger zone. I stood behind Nick. "Wyan if you send away my trucks, I can't build, that is bad business."

Wyan jabbed a finger at Nick's chest but he did not make

contact. "Why you accuse me of that?" he barked, "why you say I do that to truck?"

Nick used the finger jabbing as an excuse to move to the side. I could feel Nick's tension and I moved with him. He held up a hand to keep Wyan back. "If I can't build, I don't get paid," he paused, "I can't pay staff, if I don't get paid, Wyan."

Wyan growled and flexed his massive shoulders, "If you not pay me I make trouble, more trouble than truck!"

Nick remained composed. He didn't take his eyes of Wyan's and continued to speak calmly. "Maybe we should talk about this later, when you have relaxed a little."

I had no idea Wyan was armed but I now believe Wyan wanted Nick to fire up so he could attack him with his knife. Nick's sixth sense probably saved us both as he remained unruffled throughout the conversation. I was focused on Nick and I was unaware of the danger. Had Wyan stabbed Nick, I would have thought it was a punch and I would have stepped in to protect him. I have no doubt that I would have been stabbed next.

The size of Wyan's knife, his power and the fact that he was on meth, made for a dangerous combination. If things had sparked, there would have been a blood bath. I had nightmares about this scenario for a long time afterwards.

Luckily Nick kept us both safe by remaining relaxed and keeping his distance, but we were in trouble as Wyan wanted to attack somebody.

Made chose that moment to enter the front office with three other employees. He looked towards Wyan then kept walking towards the back of the building.

Wyan turned his attention on Made, Nick's brother-in-law, he bellowed something in Balinese then rushed over and delivered a massive right hand punch to Made's head. The sound of the blow echoed around the office. Everyone bar Nick stood stunned.

Made sprawled to the floor under the force of the blow. He hit the ground hard then flopped over and struggled to get away. He pushed back and away from Wyan—the employees he'd entered with abandoned him, they reversed themselves up against a wall.

Wyan paced up and down. He cracked his neck and rolled his shoulders then thundered and charged Made again. Nick rushed Wyan and took him out with a rugby side tackle and they both crashed to the floor. Nick spun Wyan onto his back and pinned his arms. I dove on top a moment later—it took two of us to hold him down.

Wyan kicked, struggled and screamed, and tried to break free. Nick tried to keep Wyan's arms pinned to the ground—he told me later that he knew Wyan had a knife but I still had no idea he was armed—and we did our best to hold him down but he was too strong.

Nick and Wyan struggled on the ground, they were face to face and shoulder to shoulder. Wyan had a weight advantage and an age advantage—he also had drugs shooting around his system. Nick had the advantage of being on top and having me to lend a hand, but Wyan's sheer strength kept forcing his thick neck and shoulders from the floor.

Suddenly, Nick thrust backwards. I sensed that he was trying to put distance between himself and Wyan and I relaxed and went with him, and we flew back but kept our feet. Wyan stood up and turned on us; he roared and reached behind his back. Wyan produced a ten-inch hunting knife and swung the blade at Nick and me.

Nick and I edged away from the knife and I saw Dave retreat behind a desk and Made shuffle away. The other employees found themselves trapped against the wall—somehow we had formed a semi-circle in front of Wyan. He stepped towards us and brandished the knife, swinging it from side to side in slow motion, like a cobra looking to strike. His eyes were wild and they darted back and forth in a frenzy. Wyan swung the knife at each of us in turn; the blade was wide, sharp and jagged and was a lethal looking piece of steel. Wyan would stare at somebody then move the knife on—it was like a freaky game of Russian roulette. Nobody knew who would get the bullet, but we all thought it was coming.

Wyan pointed the knife in my direction and it felt like he was debating whether to kill me. Everything seemed to slow and my mind began to race. I tried to think of a way out and realised there wasn't one; I wondered if he would stab me or move on.

I looked at the blade and noticed it was razor sharp—Bali sharp—and I wondered what damage it would do to my body. I had seen Wyan sharpen it a hundred times while he sat bored in front of the office. Wyan's eyes caught my own and I saw his craziness, it was frightening and surreal. Another fucking day in Bali, I thought.

I came to my senses and I pleaded with Wyan. "Put it down, no Wyan, put it down." My voice seemed to come from another place, from some other person. The knife moved on and I let out a deep breath. I'm sure the next person in line went through the same thing.

I have no doubt that Wyan wanted to stab someone. I'm also sure that Nick was a prime candidate, the knife hovered on him a long time, the only thing that saved us was that Wyan couldn't make up his drug-addled mind who he hated the most.

By pure, insane coincidence—and it's still difficult to believe—there happened to be a policeman in the office on the day that Wyan pulled the knife. I have a sneaking suspicion that Nick's wife may have organised this. She happened to be making a statement to the policeman at the time and she is an intelligent woman who is very protective of her husband. However I have no proof of this and when I asked Nick about it later he said he had no idea the policeman was in the building.

Either way, I have never been so glad to see a Balinese policeman in my life.

The policeman was in a back office all along. He had been brought in to solve the problem of pilfering and must have heard the commotion. The policeman pushed through the group and charged at Wyan, grabbing Wyan's knife hand. He had a gun but didn't pull it; it was probably a blessing, who knows who he would have shot. He took Wyan's knife hand firmly in his grip, stepped behind him and placed an arm about his bull neck.

Wyan stared at us, an animal deprived of his prey. He lunged forward and the policeman struggled to hold him back. The policeman screamed at Wyan in Balinese. I don't know what he said but it seemed to make him relax. The tension left Wyan's body and he slumped slightly, the policeman twisted Wyan's arm behind his back, shoving it up high. Wyan let the knife fall and it clunked to the ground. I stared at it and again wondered at the damage it would have done to a body. The policeman pulled Wyan backwards and pushed him through the front door, then loosened his grip, spun Wyan around and spoke to him harshly. Almost immediately Wyan's head slumped into his neck; he looked like an oversized child receiving a scolding.

When the policeman finished he turned his back on Wyan and marched back into the office. As soon as he was safely inside Nick screamed, "Somebody lock that fucking door!" And somebody did.

Wyan stumbled a few steps towards his motorbike then turned and raised his muscled arms above his head like a gorilla. He screamed at us through the window, climbed on his bike, and left.

We let out a collective sigh of relief. We would find out later that Wyan had spent the night smoking shabu-shabu and that he had planned to take his revenge for getting caught in the truck scam by stabbing someone.

Wyan's uncle, Rap, told us this, and when asked why he hadn't warned anybody Rap said that he was afraid Wyan would kill him if he said anything.

We all thought it was over, even Dave came out from behind his desk. Everyone spoke at a hundred miles an hour trying to put the bizarre events into some sort of perspective.

It was an odd scene and one that was about to get even weirder. Wyan's motorbike suddenly screamed back into the carpark and he rode up to the front door of the office. We all panicked. "Keep that door locked," Nick demanded, but he had no control over the policeman, who promptly walked over to the door and opened it.

Nick and I stood together and I heard him mumble, "Oh fuck." I felt the same way but I didn't say anything, I was too nervous.

The policeman stood in the door frame and exchanged a few words with Wyan, then turned and spoke to one of the staff in Indonesian. Nick must have understood the Indonesian. "Do not give him the knife. You will not give him the knife!" he yelled at the staff member. The staff member looked from Nick to the policeman and there was an obvious conflict, his boss had told him not to do something while an Indonesian policeman had told him to do it.

Nick screamed again but the policeman grunted and held out his hand. The staff member picked up the knife and handed it over and the policeman then passed the knife to Wyan.

Nick shook his head in disgust. "Fuck me," he muttered, and I almost laughed. I guess he thought the policeman had decided to side with Wyan. In the end we needn't have worried, the policeman spoke to Wyan who got back on his bike and left.

The policeman walked back into the office and he must have seen our shocked faces because he looked around, smiled and then said in English: "Don't worry he gone now. He just wanted his knife back."

There was nervous laughter all round, then Dave piped up: "Only in fucking Bali would they hand the knife back to the assailant."

There was no work done that day or for the next few days. Nick shut down the office and Dave, Nick and I went to the pub and got smashingly drunk.

Dave phoned his wife who had connections in the army, and she organised for a solider to be posted in front of the office for the next month. When Dave hung up the phone he joked, "Only in Bali would you have to hire security to protect yourself from your own security." It was to become Dave's catchphrase, but I couldn't fault the honesty of the statement.

Nick would meet Wyan again face to face so he could sack him. By all accounts everything went well, but I thought it was a crazy, brave, thing to do.

Nick told me later that Wyan had asked him why he was being sacked and he'd answered, "Wyan, you pulled a knife in my office and you threatened to kill me and my staff."

Apparently Wyan's reply was: "I'm a security guard, I'm supposed to carry a knife."

The Wyan problem was soon solved. Made was connected to a Balinese gang based in Singaraja, his brother was high up in the gang and considered to be a very dangerous man. The brother sent down a few thugs to threaten Wyan and Wyan and his gang backed down from a proposed confrontation. Again you just never know who you are dealing with in Bali.

From that point on Nick made it policy not to hire gangs into our company. We'd learnt from our mistake but we still had two gang members in our employ. Rap stayed with the company for a while but he was eventually caught with two prostitutes in one of our villas and was promptly let go.

One final gang member was harder to get rid of. He made numerous threats against Nick and our company and even tried to recruit Wyan against us. Luckily Wyan didn't like him and he used the information to get back in our good books. We got rid of him only when another company came to us about poaching him and we gladly let him go.

Eventually the trouble passed and we were able to get to a stage where we didn't need army or police protection. We no longer have security in the form of muscle and we now prefer to use connected lawyer types—a dangerous game in itself.

To this day I still see expat businessmen hiring gang thugs to work for their companies. I guess there is some sort of allure in being seen with gang members and there is, of course, the safety issue of doing business in Bali, but this is not a good course of action. Gangs are gangs and these guys are criminals and they are very dangerous—we learned this the hard way.

Yank the Yank

Living in Bali can be a little like experiencing Chinese water torture. Things happen every day that annoy you, they build and build and eventually you crack. This happens to all expats and it doesn't matter how calm a person you are.

Even the most experienced Bali hands still get ripped off. I have lived in Bali a long time and I still get ripped off on a daily basis. Nowadays I just realise it faster and ignore it more.

The other day, I went to buy a mirror for my motorbike. When I went to pay, I asked the mechanic how much it cost and the mechanic replied "Tiga puluh", slang for Rp30,000.

The cashier shook her head, however, and said, "Tidak. Enam puluh. Bule!" ("No. Rp60,000, he's a white man.") The mechanic nodded his head in agreement with her.

The cashier didn't realise I spoke a little Indonesian and I knew she had doubled my price because I'm white. I argued with her and got the price down but that was not important, I still had to come up with the energy to argue and I knew I might go through the same thing a number of times that day. The problem is that when you get ripped off on a regular basis—up to three or four times a day—it starts to wear thin.

Living and working in Indonesia can be incredibly frustrating.

There is an endless list of complaints that I could put forward: people push in, cut you off in traffic, diddle bills, etc, but the truth is it is not my country and I choose to live here. I also believe that living in Bali offers numerous advantages and that I'm incredibly lucky to have been given the opportunity to live here. My point is though, when four or five of these things happen in one day, when ten or fifteen of these things happen in one week, or when fifty or sixty of these things happen in one month, expats inevitably explode.

Every expat does this and they have different ways of expressing it but it happens on a regular basis. One friend found himself spending the night in jail because he chased down a dog with a BB gun after it tried to bite his daughter one too many times. Stupidly he chased the dog into the owner's yard and the owner had him arrested.

Another friend pushed an Indonesian barman into a swimming pool because he over-charged him. This was bad behaviour and I don't condone it, but whereas a two-week tourist might not have noticed or bothered with the over-charge, an expat will. This expat had spent hundreds of dollars in the same bar and had been ripped off by the same barman countless times ... eventually he just snapped.

I have watched expats stand and scream in the middle of busy streets, I have watched them explode irrationally at waiters or hotel staff, and I have watched them wipe off whole tables because a bill is wrong. These are instances of overreaction and rude behaviour but what is generally the case is that a collection of negative occurrences have built up over time and the expat has just been pushed too far.

As recently as a month ago an expat associate was sitting in a bar when a young girl asked him to buy bracelets for the hundredth time. The expat told the girl he would buy a bracelet if she gave him a receipt. This was a stupid and demeaning thing to say, and I personally would have acted differently, but his defence was that the same girl had bothered him every day over a three-month period.

An Australian girl with an Indonesian boyfriend happened to be sitting in the same bar. She overheard the expat and called him a cruel fucking idiot. The expat told her in no uncertain terms to mind her own business. The Australian girl then prompted her Indonesian boyfriend to get his gang together and they beat the expat and his two friends with bricks and motorcycle helmets.

The expats were in their sixties while the gang and the Australian girl were in their twenties but apparently the Australian girl felt they deserved the beating. She egged her boyfriend on and gave the expats a serve-you-right mouthful when she left.

The expats that I spoke to felt that the Australian girl should live in Bali for a year and then evaluate if what was said to the girl was cruel. You can be the judge as to who was in the wrong, and perhaps you would say everyone, but the fact is stuff like this happens all the time.

Expats do act stupidly, and spitefully, towards Indonesians, and for the most part it is because they get sick of being scammed or taken advantage of. I am not saying this is the correct course of action, I don't believe it is, but it does happen.

The other thing expats do is fight each other. Exasperation at the system, the country or the people builds and rather than take it out on the local populace these expats harbour their frustrations. Sometimes these expats meet and two time-bombs collide.

I must have had a bad day, week or month on the particular occasion when I lost my cool but luckily I chose a deserving bastard to lose it on.

Wade is a conman. He survives by befriending tourists then, after qualifying that their stay in Bali is short, he borrows money from them. Unsuspecting tourists hand over the cash, a meeting is set for the following day, then Wade disappears until the tourists leave Bali. This is one of Wade's scams and I know there are more, but I'm using this one as an explanation because I have been given verification that he has done this on a number of occasions.

I have never had much time for Wade. When I first came to Bali I heard a story about him that convinced me to keep my distance.

Billy, my brother, is the kind of guy that likes to get amongst it. He would much prefer to live the same way as the locals than be stuck with a group of expats.

Long before I came to live in Bali, Wade and Billy lived in the same complex, which consisted of ten *kosts*, or apartments, that surrounded a large grass area. Wade's *kost* happened to be a few doors down from Billy's but the two didn't socialise.

One night Billy woke to a girl screaming and he went to investigate. The screams happened to be coming from Wade's *kost*. Billy walked up the front steps of the *kost* and banged on the door. Wade answered the door drunk and berated Billy for disturbing him. Billy looked past Wade and saw an Indonesian girl in the corner. She was sobbing and it was obvious from her injuries that she'd been beaten.

Billy grabbed Wade by the scruff of the neck, dragged him down his stairs, threw him onto the grass then challenged Wade to hit him the same way he had hit the girl. Wade remained on the ground and refused to fight.

Billy left Wade and walked into his house, he collected the beaten girl and carried her back to his home. Billy's Indonesian wife cared for the girl until the morning and the next day Billy and his wife helped her get home to her village. Wade moved out of the compound soon after the event.

When I first came to live in Bali, Billy told me this story and pointed Wade out to me. For obvious reasons I wanted nothing to do with the guy. Wade is American and and his face is pockmarked with very bad acne scars but because I had only seen him from a distance, I was unaware of his skin problems. When I had my run-in with him he was in his mid-thirties, stocky and fit.

*　*　*

Billy and I decided to walk from Kuta beach to Poppies One for a beer. Halfway to our destination, Billy dragged me into a roadside bar that just happened to be Wade's hangout. We sat at a table a metre off the road and ordered a beer.

Not long after, Wade rode up on his motorbike. I do not know what sort of relationship Billy and Wade had after the incident at the *kost* but Wade seemed comfortable enough to stop. Billy introduced me to Wade and I got up from the table and shook his hand. It was then that I noticed his acne scars.

Wade looked sick, like he had caught some weird tropical facial disease. I didn't mean to offend him but I asked, "Are you alright, what's wrong with your face?"

Wade didn't seem to take it well. "I'm going to join you," he said, then went and parked his motorbike. When he returned to the table he looked at Billy and asked. "Did you hear what he just said to me?"

Billy shrugged, "No." He didn't have much time for Wade.

I realised my mistake. I didn't care if I hurt Wade's feelings but I didn't want a confrontation. I stuck out my hand again, "Look mate, I'm sorry. Your face is scarred and I thought you were sick, it was an honest mistake."

Wade refused to shake my hand. He ordered a beer, walked around the table and sat beside me. He put his face close to mine and fixed me with an angry stare. "Why did you say that to me?" he asked.

I sensed Wade was trying to intimidate me. I held his gaze but my chair backed onto the step leading to the road. If Wade had swung at me I would have toppled backwards; I was in a vulnerable position. "Hey mate, I said I'm sorry, OK. I didn't mean anything by it, I genuinely thought you were sick."

Wade took a sip on his beer and continued to stare. "What's your problem, mate?" he asked.

I laughed, hoping it would ease the tension, "Listen mate, there is not much more I can do. I have apologised, alright."

I smiled at him and moved my chair forward an inch. "I'm not laughing at your face, it's just when Americans say mate it sounds stupid," I replied. "No offence, maaate."

Wade squared his shoulders. "Fucking Aussies," he snarled, and continued to try and menace me. He picked up my cigarette packet and took out a smoke, then used my lighter. "There are too many fucking Aussies in Bali. You fucking Aussies think you own Bali."

I leaned forward and held his gaze. I'd had enough. "Listen mate, I will make this simple. Don't take my cigarettes, don't try and intimidate me, and as for Australians taking over countries, take a look at your own country."

Billy interrupted. He reached across the table and offered his hand to Wade. "No more," he said, and waited for Wade to accept the handshake.

Wade took Billy's hand; he twisted his hand over and strained to dominate the grip. Billy locked his wrist.

Billy and Wade stared at each other. They had their own battle of wills and I could see the hatred in Wade's eyes. I guessed he hadn't forgotten the night at the *kost*. Wade tightened his grip and yanked Billy towards him. Billy gave a little then then yanked back hard.

Wade flew forward and caught himself on the table. He gripped the edge and gave his best pull. Billy didn't flinch; he yanked back with his considerable strength and pulled Wade across the table.

Wade let go of Billy's hand and pushed himself up. "What the fuck, dude?" he asked.

Billy stared him down. "You want to make trouble, fucker?" he asked.

Wade puffed out his chest and pointed a finger at Billy, "What are you going to fucking do, man?"

I had seen and heard enough, Billy and I had been having a quiet drink and Wade had invited himself over. Maybe Wade was having a bad day but he was certainly trying to make trouble, he'd tried to intimidate me and he was trying to intimidate my little brother. Billy can handle himself, and he does not need me to stick up for him, but I'd had just about as much as I was going to take from the obnoxious American.

I didn't like Wade, I didn't like that he hit women and I didn't like how he made his living. I admit that what I did next wasn't really fair but to be honest I just thought, fuck it.

"Hey, Wade," I called out.

Wade turned to me with a snarl on his face, "What the fuck do you—"

I didn't give Wade a chance to finish. I wacked him and I wacked him hard. He flew backwards, and down he smashed through the wooden chair he'd been sitting on moments before.

I knew I had committed myself. Wade was younger, bigger, fitter and stronger than me. He also lived in Bali and I didn't want any retribution. I had set myself on a course of action and I knew I had to make a good example, so I followed Wade down and threw punches all the way.

He hit the ground and I landed on top of him. My left hand found his throat and I drilled two hard punches into his pockmarked face. His lip split and his nose broke, blood sprayed up at me and he coughed but I hadn't finished. I wanted Wade unconscious. I smacked Wade again then lifted my arm for the knockout blow but felt myself hefted up and backwards.

At the time I did not know who had grabbed me and I struggled to free myself, but whoever held me had a professional grip like a policeman. They also happened to be very strong.

My legs lifted off the ground. I writhed but could not break free.

"Sorry mate, I can't let you go further," said a rich Aussie voice in my ear.

I looked down at Wade and watched as he began to pick himself up. There were large splinters of wood all around—the remnants of the chair—and I was worried Wade would pick up a sharp piece of wood and use it against me. I kicked, squirmed and screamed and then suddenly the big Aussie that held me let me go.

I hit the ground running and dove for a stake. When I had one in my hand I got up and tried to charge Wade with it. "I'll fucking kill you," I screamed at the top of my lungs.

Wade turned and started to run and I made to chase him. The big Aussie yanked me back and enclosed me in his arms. "Enough!" he said, forcefully.

I watched Wade run down the road and away from me. The Aussie was right, it was enough. I knew that Wade wouldn't be back.

Fallen Angel

I'm often asked by young male tourists whether as an old hand in Bali I can help them meet an Indonesian prostitute. I even helped a friend's virgin nephew get himself a working girl one night. I saw this as community service—the guy was twenty-one years old and he had never had sex.

Physically there was nothing wrong with Warren. He was handsome, and on the few occasions that I had spoken to him he'd come across as intelligent. To my mind he should have been bonking his twenty-one-year-old heart out, so I put his problem down to shyness.

I was drinking with Warren and his uncle, Martin, one evening, and when Martin went to the toilet Warren asked if I could help him.

"What's up?" I asked, only too happy to help. Warren was a nice kid who was always polite.

Warren took a quick glance around to make sure nobody was listening, then leaned across the table. "Can you help me meet a prostitute?" he asked shyly.

I laughed. I was expecting the question. "No," I said.

Warren sat back in his chair and blushed. "OK," he said.

I felt sorry for him and motioned him forward. "Look, I can't help you meet a prostitute but I will help you meet a working girl. It may not seem like it, but there is a bit of a difference."

Warrens face lit up, he took a deep breath. "Thank you," he said, and smiled.

I held up a hand and stopped him, "Not so fast, big fella. First you have to tell me why you want to meet a girl."

Warren looked around again to make sure nobody could hear—he almost climbed up the table to whisper to me. "I'm a virgin," he said. "I came on this holiday to have sex, and I have tried since I got here, but I can't meet girls. This is my last night and I go home tomorrow, can you please help?"

Warren was desperate and I didn't want him taking home some skank off the street so I decided to help. "You've come to the right place," I said, and smiled.

Warren's uncle came out of the toilet. "Please don't tell Uncle Martin," he pleaded quickly.

I winked at him, "I won't say a word."

I cleared it with Martin at the very next opportunity and he was happy for me to help his nephew. He also swore not to let on that he knew. Martin made his excuses a short time later and disappeared and I took Warren to a little place that I knew.

I found Warren a nice girl his own age and organised the price, which dropped dramatically when I mentioned he was a virgin. I also gave her a lecture about making Warren wear a condom. I then gave Warren a lecture about treating the girl with respect, and wearing a condom, and walked them back to Warren's hotel room where I said goodbye and wished them a nice night.

The next day, Warren thanked me profusely and again made me swear never to tell his uncle. He told me he'd had the most wonderful night, that the girl had stayed the whole evening, and that he'd given her a large tip before she left. Warren never found out that I had cleared it with his uncle first.

(I know a woman that works six days a week in a laundry so that she can support her child. She is a single mother and there is no such thing as social security benefits in Indonesia. Every now and again when things are tight and she needs to buy schoolbooks or pay the rent or just buy something for herself, this woman goes out and meets a man. If I had to, and for want of a better term, I would classify this woman as a working girl, not a prostitute.)

* * *

One night, several months after helping Warren, I struck up a conversation with a group of young Australians in a bar. While we were talking, one of the young guys, a good-looking twenty-two-year old, asked, "You've lived in Indonesia for a long time, can you tell me how I can meet an Indonesian prostitute?"

The young Aussie guy, Luke, took me aback; he was a very good looking bloke in a young Brad Pitt kind of way. He was a fit and strong surfer type with white blonde hair down to his shoulders. He was the kind of guy you didn't want to go to a nightclub with as he would take home the best-looking girl every time.

Why he wanted to sleep with an Indonesian prostitute when he could have any girl he set his sights on was beyond me, so I posed the question to Luke and his friends. "Listen mate, and I'm not saying this in a gay way, but you could have any girl you want, you're a good-looking bloke. Why the hell do you want to sleep with an Indonesian prostitute?"

Luke laughed and I instantly liked the guy, he wasn't big-headed, despite looking like a high school girl's wet dream. "It's just something I have always wanted to do," he said, and smirked.

One of Luke's mates thumped him on the shoulder and joined the conversation. "It's all he's talked about since we arrived in Bali."

Luke turned and thumped his friend back. "Fuck off! It's not all I've talked about," he smiled, then laughed like Beavis and Butthead. "Well, yeah, most of the time."

I thought for a moment. Warren had been different, he was a virgin and he obviously needed help getting over the hurdle, but Luke was something else. He was confident, handsome and blonde. I knew that Indonesian girls, and Indonesian working girls alike, would throw themselves at him. There was something I was missing. Luke should not have needed my help. "OK," I said warily, "I can do it, but first I need to ask what sort of girl you want to meet?"

Luke smiled, showed me his perfect white teeth, and came out with the nasty truth. "The dirtier the better," he replied, "I want the biggest, baddest, hooker in Bali."

The answer intrigued me and funnily enough I knew just the girl, but I didn't mention this to him. "Why?" I asked, interested. "Why would you want that?"

Luke shrugged he looked around to his mates for the answer,

one of his friends shoved him, "Tell him what you told us," he said.

Luke turned back to me and smiled shyly. "It's just what I've always wanted," he said.

"OK," I said and paused, trying to give myself time to think. "If that's what you want."

I looked to Luke's mates for support. "Is he serious?" I asked, hoping one of them would tell me Luke was joking.

Luke's mates giggled, pushed each other playfully as they tried to answer first. "Yep," two of them said in unison. "That's how he likes 'em," chimed another.

I decided to give it one more shot for the sake of Luke's future psyche. If Luke had have been ugly or shy I probably wouldn't have bothered, but Luke looked like he'd just stepped out of a sunglasses add in a Rip Curl magazine and the girl I had in mind was a soul destroying demon that had been taught her craft in the dark heart of Sumatra by witches and gypsies. It wasn't exactly a match made in heaven and I felt that I might be committing myself to the fires of hell if I allowed her to stick her claws into the young man's character.

* * *

Angel is about thirty and she is petite, pretty and poised. When a man arrives at her place of work she will take him by the hand and lead him demurely into the Promised Land. She will close the door, ask him to lie down and then she will disrobe. She will then step into her bath and shower and wash herself in full view.

When Angel has finished her scrub she will render the john naked, clasp him by the hand, then lead him into her bath. She will then gently clean him down with warm soapy water and dry him with a fluffy towel. When bath time is over, Angel will take the customer to her bed and proceed to massage all his troubles away. And she is a wonderful masseuse. It's hard to stay awake when she plays a symphony on your shoulders with her strong, sublime fingers.

Angel will massage her client all over then sit astride his chest and ask softly in a sweet, demure voice whether he is OK. Her client will look up through hazy, sleepy eyes and see a beautiful Indonesian princess sitting naked astride his warm and oiled body. Then Angel will smile, lean down into his face and whisper, "Do you want more?"

Angel's client might hear the change in her voice … it will seem somehow huskier. He will look up to see her petite firm breasts hovering inches above his chest and he'll reply with his voice choking on the words, "Yes, I want more."

Then all hell breaks loose.

* * *

Angel was a legend in Bali, I kept hearing her name but nobody would tell me anything. I would ask about Angel, and the only reply I would receive was a knowing smile, or a, "If you haven't been there, you will never know" comment. One night I bit the bullet and went to visit Angel. I have never been the same since.

Unfortunately, except for what I have just written, I cannot divulge any more. I will, however, say this. When you leave after a visit with Angel, your legs seem hollow and it is a chore to walk, a smile is plastered to your face, and the world seems a better place. When you reach home, your night's dreams are filled with jasmine smoke, hot sex flashes and visions of Angel riding you hard like a woman riding a stallion in a storm.

Angel was an experience, a happening, an initiation and a rite of passage, she was an earthquake wrapped up in a five-foot-two body.

Angel was Heaven sent, ethereal and brutally sexual; she was an athletic contortionist with zero inhibition.

That's about the best I can do, but a better description would be: Angel is a fallen Angel.

This was where I took the young Australian that night.

Angel greeted me at her door like an old friend, she went to kiss me on the lips but I turned my head and offered my cheek. It was not a wise thing to let the baddest hooker in Bali kiss you on the lips; you never know where that mouth has been.

I introduced Angel to the young Australian and she seemed pleased. I felt like a man handing a virgin to a vampire. Angel took Luke by the hand and led him down the passageway.

"Angel, go easy on him please," I blurted.

She ignored me and, smiling, she gently guided the young boy through her bedroom door. At the last moment Angel turned, gave me a wink, and my heart sank.

*   *   *

I turned to the young man's friends and shook my head. "He will never be the same again," I said sadly.

Luke's friends looked at me like I was some sort of weirdo so to change the mood a little I clapped my hands together and said. "Right then, now that's done, let's go get a massage and a hand job."

The boy's jaws dropped. "Where?" they asked.

"Why, it's just across the street," I said happily.

I walked the boys through the whole happy ending experience offered in Bali. It really isn't that complicated: you choose a girl, she gives you a massage, and then she makes a sly gesture at your crotch and asks, "You want?"

If you say you do, she will then negotiate a price.

You should always let her say her price first and know that it will be exorbitant, then give her your own price, she will try and get the price up by telling you happy endings are not allowed in the massage parlour. This is generally a lie, but they all say it and you have to be careful as some places in Bali do not give happy endings. The simple rule is, if she offers, then she is allowed.

Negotiate the price, get the job done, take a warm shower and be on your way.

I explained all this to the boys in a flash and we organised to meet about an hour later so we could pick up Luke. I had a massage and then I sat in the lounge and waited for the young Aussie guys to come down.

Happy ending massage joints are great opportunities for avid people-watchers like me. The girls in these places are quite diverse and they generally fit into three categories.

The first are young women that do not want to sell themselves fully into prostitution; these women come to the big city and look for proper work but they need to survive while they are job hunting.

The next group seems to be women that have just come down from Java seeking work but they are not confident enough with their English skills to find a job or to work the clubs. They work in these massage joints to earn a little money so they can support themselves and their child—a lot of these women have given birth recently and been dumped by their Javanese boyfriends—they hope to learn English and/or meet a Westerner to marry.

The third group is generally made up of married woman who are seeking a little extra cash on the side. I have no idea if their husbands know what they do during the day but it wouldn't surprise me if they did.

The clientele is not as diverse as one may think and it's probably made up more of Indonesians than Westerners. The Indonesians that visit these places appear mostly to be middle-aged, middle-class, married men seeking a little release and freedom after work. The practise is definitely Asian, and although, at first glance it may not seem like it, I'm inclined to think it has a justifiable purpose. The places are generally clean, they are well organised and the massages are genuine. For a married man they offer an opportunity for release that does not involve prostitutes, affairs, or the chance of catching an STD.

* * *

One by one the young Aussie guys descended the steps of the massage joint. I was pleased when they all walked down the steps holding the hands of the respective masseurs—I remember thinking it was really cute.

The boys and I crossed the road to rescue their mate from Angel's evil clutches. When Luke walked out of the front door of Angel's Den of Iniquity he was a devastating sight. He grinned from ear to ear, walked with a shuffling gait, his belt was open and hung down and his shirt was on backwards. He raised his hand in a gesture of greeting and mumbled a weak, "Hi guys."

I felt terrible, Luke had become a shell of his former self, and he looked like someone had sucked out his soul. I knew the symptoms well enough but feared one so young would not survive a session with Angel.

Luke's mates carried him to his motorbike; they placed him on the seat and set his hands on the handlebars. He looked like a drunk from a Seventies cartoon and I was worried that he would not be able to ride. We drove sedately back to the pub where we had first met.

By the time we had arrived at the pub Luke had perked up somewhat. He thanked me, bought me a beer and we all sat down to compare notes.

First I asked him if he was OK and he assured me he was. Next I asked, "How did it go?" Luke looked me squarely in the eyes and I could see they now sparkled with the knowledge of ages, a knowledge only received by those who have experienced Angel. I could see that Luke had come of age.

I felt a little sad at the innocence lost but I also felt proud of my young Jedi. He had stepped bravely into the lions den, he had walked in the valley of the shadow of death, and although he seemed a little exhausted, he had survived and remained intact. Luke said one word and I believe it summed up his experience completely.

"Wow!" he said, and then he shook his head and took a sip of his beer. "Wow!"

I was unsure if I had done the right thing but I nodded knowingly.

From The Mouths of Babes

Strange things happen in Bali. This morning I received a phone call from a panicky prostitute. She woke me up at five o'clock so she could ask for my help. The phone call was from a girl named Lita. She knows Fish, and she knows that Fish and I are friends.

Lita was leaving a nightclub with a client when she noticed the security guards were surrounding somebody lying on the floor. When Lita went over to investigate she found Fish passed out drunk at their feet. She asked the security if there was a problem. They looked down at Fish and asked, "Do you know this man?"

Lita told the security that she did. "Good," said the security, "then he is your problem. Take him home, we want to close up."

Lita tried to wake Fish but she couldn't. She asked her client if he would help carry Fish from the nightclub. The client declined to help; he did not want to get involved. He tried to drag Lita away but she refused to leave Fish to the mercy of the security and eventually the client became angry and left. Lita went back to the security and pleaded for help. After a lot of begging she managed to enlist one of them to help her carry Fish outside the club.

Once outside she realised she could not leave Fish asleep on the side of the road and so she hailed a taxi. Lita and the security guard pushed Fish into the back seat of the car but Lita had a problem, she had no money to pay the driver. She went through Fish's pockets and found no money, but she did find his phone. She trawled through Fish's numbers and found mine.

I woke up after the second call, picked up the phone, and heard a distressed sounding Lita on the other end. "Mal my name Lita, I friend Fish. I think we meet before ya?"

I did remember Lita. Fish had introduced her about a month earlier and mentioned that she was more of a friend than a prostitute to him.

Their relationship had started as a work thing but they had become close. They referred to each other as brother and sister and while they were at the Kuta clubs they tried to keep an eye on one another. I am generally dubious about this sort of relationship but Fish swore Lita was honest and a good friend.

Lita is thirtyish, she is intelligent, bubbly and pretty, but Lita is also tired. The years working in the clubs have taken their toll. She spends six nights a week in clubs and drinks way too much.

Lita is like most of the prostitutes in and around Kuta but she has one thing that sets her apart, she has one of the sexiest voices I have ever heard. The first time I met her I was driven to compliment her on her voice, she speaks in a whiskey-soaked soft way like a woman on the edge of orgasm. I found it incredibly sexy and I told her so. This is probably why Lita remembered me and why she looked for me in Fish's phone; it was certainly why I remembered her, her voice was unmistakable, even at five in the morning.

I had just woken from a deep sleep and had no idea why

Lita was calling me. I looked at the phone and recognised Fish's number and guessed there might be a problem. "Good morning Lita, yes I remember you darling. What's wrong?"

Like most Indonesians Lita was direct and to the point. "I have difficulty Mal. I in taxi with Fish, he very drunk and he sleep nightclub. I worry for him Mal, I have no money. Can you help me?"

I rubbed sleep from my eyes, "Is everything OK?" I asked, trying to come to my senses. "What happened to Fish?"

"Fish OK but he very drunk, I need money Mal. Fish have no money and man taxi angry to me."

I am always wary when Indonesian prostitutes ask me for money, especially ones I barely know. "Lita, can I speak to Fish?" I asked.

There was a pause and then I heard the muffled sounds of Lita trying to wake up Fish, she came back on the line. "Fish *mabuk*, Lita cannot wake. I have no money and taxi driver angry, please help me."

This was not the first time I had been woken early because Fish had got himself into trouble. Ever since a dispute with his ex-girlfriend he'd been on a downhill run. The ex-girlfriend was not content with taking all Fish's money, she was now calling all his contacts in Australia and telling them that he'd bashed and beaten her. She was also harassing him daily by text and threatening to make trouble with Indonesian immigration.

Fish had developed a drinking problem and I had received a similar call a week earlier. He had fallen asleep in front of a bar on Legian Street and was lucky an Indonesian associate of ours recognised him. He was also lucky to still have his wallet.

I gave Lita my address and told her to bring Fish over in the taxi, I said that I would organise the fare.

Having paid off the driver I tried to give Lita fifty thousand for her trouble but she shook her head and refused to take it. "Fish my friend too, Mal. I not need money for look after him."

Prostitutes are looked down on by a lot of people but being a working girl doesn't stop them from being human. Lita is a good example, she has done a lot to protect a friend and make sure he is safe.

Later in the day when Fish and Lita woke, we all sat down to chat and give Fish a hard time for being a drunk. I discovered that Lita loved to talk; the conversation we had was interesting so I have decided to include it.

I asked Lita where she was from in Indonesia—this question is important to Indonesians. Indonesia is a large place with many islands, cultures and regional dialects, and Indonesians place a great significance on their place of birth. They love to talk about their origins and their home city or village.

Lita told us that she was from Surabaya, the second largest city in Java. Surabaya is a polluted port town that I have visited in the past, and like all port towns it has a seedy side. When I mentioned this to Lita she decided to tell us her history.

She told us her mother had died in 2004 when she was twenty-four and that at the time her father was a successful tailor. He employed five people in a large shop and Lita worked in the shop with her father. She has a little sister that was nine at the time of her mother's death and Lita's father scaled down his business so that he could take care of his youngest daughter.

Lita said she had helped out with her sister and the shop but things were difficult. Her father continued to grieve for his wife and he had problems at work. Eventually the business failed. Lita's father lost all his employees and he had to move to a smaller shop. Her father took her aside one day and told her he could not afford to look after her anymore and said he was having problems paying to send his youngest daughter to school. He told her that she would need to help and asked her to find work in a complex.

She was given no choice, her father asked and she obeyed. This is the Indonesian way, the woman must follow the man and the daughter must follow the father. "Complex" is the word Lita used for a brothel.

She told us she had to work very hard at the complex, she was expected to sleep with seven or eight men a night and if she complained she was beaten. She was paid Rp150,000 (about fifteen Australian dollars) a time to sleep with a man and said that Rp50,000 went to the complex and Rp100,000 went to her father and her young sister's schooling. She struggled to retain any of the money for herself. She said that if she wanted to leave the complex she was expected to pay Rp5,000,000 (approximately 520 Australian dollars) to the owner

Lita said this was common for all the girls in the complex and that threats to families were delivered nightly to stop the girls from running away. She said that the threats were followed through with and she was often told that if she left without paying her fine her father and younger sister would be beaten.

She worked in the complex for three years until her father

realised he could not run his small business anymore and decided to sell. After pleading with him her father used some of the money from the sale of the shop to buy Lita's freedom and sent her to work in Bali. She's worked as a call girl in Bali ever since. She told us that it was far better than working in the complex because she has her freedom and she can sometimes buy things for herself, and she doesn't miss being beaten or being forced to sleep with up to eight men a night.

Lita sends half the money she earns back to her father and her sister, but said that sometimes her sister rings when she needs new shoes or a dress and this gives her a headache because she knows she has to work harder that month.

When I asked her if her father works she said he doesn't, he has never gotten over his wife's death and spends all his time looking after the youngest child. She said she would soon be very happy as her sister would finish her school in a few months and she would no longer have to pay for her. She said her sister had asked if she could go to university but that she had refused, she told her she could not afford it.

Hard luck stories are common in Indonesia, you hear them all the time and this is but one prostitute's tale.

Not all of Bali's prostitutes have such hard luck stories though. Some, like Ira, choose their profession because it is an easy way to make money and get ahead. Some come from very good homes yet they work so they can afford university or to buy a house or to further their financial situation, and for them prostitution is purely a business transaction.

Then there are girls that work because they'd prefer to meet and marry a Westerner. There are numerous situations and circumstances that send girls into prostitution, although most involve poverty.

Pool Hi-jinks

Josh was a good kid and from the moment we met we got along. He was twenty-one but looked seventeen; he was tall, had boyish good looks, was well mannered and was one of the most switched-on young guys I have ever met.

When he told me his life story I figured his upbringing had something to do with his maturity. He had grown up in some of Europe's trendiest nightclubs, surrounded by the rich and famous. Josh's friend Rick was different, however. He had a way about him that just didn't gel with me. He was also older than Josh by about ten years and I couldn't see the connection.

Josh and Rick were rich kids from privileged backgrounds. Josh's father owned a string of nightclubs on the Isle of Man and Josh had been partying in them since he was fifteen. His father had exiled him from the island after he stole somebody's Porsche and crashed it joy riding and Josh was spending his banishment travelling the world. Somewhere along the line he hooked up with Rick. Rick's father was a retired pilot who spent most of his time in his mansion on the island of Madagascar.

Josh and Rick told me they had met travelling—they both wanted to learn to surf and so they rented a villa from me that was situated close to Uluwatu. Every now and again I would run into one, or both, of them in Kuta.

Josh would ask me about Bali and I would give him information on where to eat and party. He was intelligent but he was young and new to Bali and I didn't mind helping as we got along well. Rick was friendly enough but I found him difficult to communicate with, he came across as a spoilt guy whose only interest was what you could do for him.

I was watching the football in a pub one early Sunday afternoon when I received a phone call from Josh. I answered but I wasn't happy because it was my day off. All I needed was a work-related call during one of the most important games of the season.

Josh sounded panicked. "Mal, I need your help."

"What's wrong?" I asked, dreading a leaky pipe or broken TV antenna.

"Rick is in the hospital, he drowned in the villa pool and I think he might be dead!"

The noise in the pub was loud and I wanted time to think. Shit, I thought, give me the leaky pipe. "Josh, I can't hear you, stay on the line, I'm going to walk outside. Do not hang up, OK?"

I made my way out of the pub and into the carpark. "OK, Josh, are you still with me?"

Josh didn't hesitate. "I think Rick may be dead or he could be brain damaged. He drowned last night, we are at the hospital and we had to get an ambulance!"

My first thought was liability. Bad I know, but I was unsure of the insurance situation at our villas and I had visions of some rich kid's dad flying over to Bali with his lawyers in tow. "Is Rick alive? What happened? How did he drown?" I asked.

I could hear Josh breathing heavily down the phone. "Fuck, fuck, it's bad," he stammered. "I don't know, I pulled him out of the water and we had to wait for an ambulance. I don't know. Are you coming here?"

I walked to my motorbike. "I'm on my way but I need information, is Rick alive?" Liability or not, I didn't want Rick to die.

"I don't know. He is in the hospital and they won't let me in." Josh swore a long line of fucks and worked himself into a frenzy. "Rick drowned and I don't know what to do. Please come here, we took E while we were in the pool, you have to come now!"

My mind raced, the boys were on drugs when the accident occurred. That meant I needed proof to avoid liability.

"I don't know if Rick is still alive. Please come, they won't tell me anything."

"Who won't tell you anything Josh?" I asked.

"We revived him by the pool. Two Aussie nurses helped but I'm not allowed inside."

"Josh relax and speak slowly, where are you?" I climbed on my bike but didn't start the engine. "Josh listen, look for a sign or ask someone. I will come but I need your location."

"We are at the International Hospital. The sign says BIMC ... I think it is near Sanur."

"OK, Josh, I know where it is. Now listen, I'm on my bike so you won't be able to call me, I will get there as fast as possible and I'm sure Rick will be OK."

I wanted to make one stop on the way. It may sound callous

but I wanted Josh to calm down and I wanted him to tell me the truth. I decided to stop and buy beer and cigarettes.

I arrived at the hospital fifteen minutes later. When I arrived I saw Josh sitting out front with four people: three young guys about his age and an older woman. I recognised her and my heart sank.

Mary had purchased a villa from our company a couple of years previously and she had proved to be nothing but trouble. She was an Australian nurse who had been coming to Bali quite regularly for the past three years. She was in her mid-forties, overweight and a heavy drinker; she also liked the company of young Balinese men. She and her friends would come to Bali twice a year on triple-S tours.

Everyone in the company knew her reasons for buying the villa in such an isolated location. It was hard to miss the group of middle-aged women frolicking in the pool with their young Balinese studs.

None of this would have mattered if Mary hadn't fallen for one of her sycophants. She had fallen madly in love and she happened to be going through stage three of the Divide and Conquer Scam when I met her at the hospital (see end of chapter for the four-stage Divide and Conquer Scam). Mary's boyfriend fed her false information and she believed whatever her young lover told her. The boyfriend had convinced Mary that she was in danger of losing her villa unless he handled her paperwork and her villa was placed under his control.

Mary was also a gossip who enjoyed email and she decided to share the boyfriends' false information with all of our past clients.

Unfortunately, she forgot to mention that she received her legal advice from a Balinese gigolo. This caused immeasurable damage but it wasn't the first time and Mary was not the only one to be duped.

Suffice to say, Mary was not one of my favourite people and I had no wish to hand her a negligence suit on a silver platter. I knew I had to get her on side or I risked the company being dragged through the mud in the Indonesian courts.

I called Josh to one side and I offered him a beer, which he took gratefully. I explained that I wanted to speak to Mary alone so I could assess the situation. I said that Mary would tell me the truth but she may be reluctant to talk if he was around. I said I would share any information I received with him.

I went over to Mary, offered her a beer, and sat down next to her. "You look like you've had a rough night." Mary took the beer. "Yeah, you could say that."

"Listen mate, I just want to thank you for all that you have done and —"

"It's my job," she interrupted. "I'm a nurse, it's what we do."

I nodded. "Yeah, I was married to a nurse for a long time and I worked in a hospital for a while. I know what you guys do and I have nothing but respect for nurses and the profession."

This seemed to win Mary over; she took a sip of beer and sighed. "It's not something I wanted to happen on my holiday though."

I took out my smokes and offered one to her. "Mary I need a favour," I said. "I need us to forget about business until we get this sorted, it won't do either of us any good to muddy this problem with what's going on at your villa."

Mary checked to see if I was serious. "I agree with you. This is far more important at the moment."

I respected Mary's attitude and I felt relieved. "Thank you," I said, then asked, "how is he, what's your professional opinion?"

"I don't hold much hope. Rick is young and he is very fit but he died that many times. My opinion? I think his brain will be irreparably damaged."

"How did you get involved?" I asked, and looked over at the young guys waiting for Josh in front of the hospital. "Did they come and get you?"

Mary shook her head. "We were at the pool when it happened and we kept him alive for two hours while we waited for the ambulance."

I could sense Mary needed to talk. She went on to tell me that her and her friend, another Australian nurse, had spent two hours keeping Rick alive through resuscitation. She told me that he'd died numerous times beside the pool and on the way to the hospital and that the doctors and nurses at the BIMC were struggling to keep him alive as we spoke.

She told me that the ambulance they'd arrived in had not only taken two hours to reach the scene, and another hour to get to the hospital, but that it had been ill equipped and she and her friend had reverted to hands-on techniques to keep Rick going.

Whatever I thought of Mary I could not fault her for what she was doing, this was her holiday and she was spending it working and saving a young man's life. Mary and her friend had done their job, they had kept Rick alive and made sure he arrived at a hospital.

I mentioned this to Mary and she replied, 'There is no way I would leave my patients side until I knew that I had done everything I could do. I'm in this until the end, I'm a nurse."

I thanked her again and told her that I thought she and her friend were heroes. I meant it, I have no doubt Rick would not be alive without the dedication that these two women showed to their profession and to another human being. I asked if she had said any of this to Josh and she told me she hadn't.

I walked over to Josh and passed him a beer. "Josh I need to know something and I need you to trust me."

Josh must have heard the seriousness in my voice, he pulled his head from his hands and looked up at me, "I trust you," he said, and I felt like a prick.

I turned on the seat so that Josh and I were face to face. "On the phone you said you were doing Es. That's okay, I couldn't give a fuck, but if you are on E and something bad does happen ..." I let the statement hang.

Josh was a smart guy, I knew he could work it out he looked at me wide-eyed and trusting. I could tell he was running possible scenarios through his mind.

I saw his Josh's eyes water over and passed him a lit cigarette. Josh took a drag, "You mean if Rick dies?"

I placed a hand on Josh's shoulder, "That's the worst scenario but it doesn't have to go that far," I said. "Mate, they will probably do all sorts of tests and you and your friends could be in deep shit, do you understand?"

Josh took a deep drag and exhaled over his shoulder, I could sense him trying to act mature, "I understand." he said, quietly.

I continued. I had practised the speech on the ride to the hospital. I felt like a dodgy bastard but I thought it was a good way to get Josh to admit that Rick had been on drugs. "If you were on Es we may need to act fast. Indonesia is not the place to get busted. Do you have any drugs on you?"

Josh paused and thought about his answer. "No," he said eventually, "I ditched them already. I emptied them in one of the drains, they're gone."

"Don't fucking bullshit me," I said.

Josh leaned away, he raised his hands. "I'm not bullshitting, Mal. I threw them away, I dumped 'em in a drain up at the villas."

I lowered my voice, "OK, well done, no one will find them right?"

Josh still had his hands up, "Mal, I swear they're gone mate," he ran his fingers through his hair. "Fuck, I wouldn't lie."

I gave Josh a smile to reassure him, "Okay, I had to ask. Now we have to worry about your mates."

Josh looked at me surprised, "They're staunch man, you don't have to worry about them."

"Josh let me finish, for all we know the doctors have already been in touch with the police."

Josh grabbed my arm and stopped me, he gestured at his friends. "They're firm man."

I looked into his eyes; I could see he trusted them. "I believe you, we just have to be sure you all have the same story."

Josh smiled at me, "Yeah man, it's not the first time I've been in trouble. Shit, I feel like I'm talking to my dad."

I ignored the comment. "I have to make a few phone calls. I have to let someone know and we may need a lawyer," I pointed over to Josh's friends. "Clear it with them. Let them know that I know about the drugs."

Josh looked over at his friends, "Mal, I know you are trying to help but I don't want to say anything, we made a pact before we came to the hospital."

"Mate, you have to be with me, nothing bad, just forward planning. The person I am going to call is my brother. You can trust him. I need your friends to be honest and tell me the facts."

Josh stubbed out his cigarette and finished off his beer. I could see him using the moment to decide whether to let his friends know and could sense the choice was difficult.

I opened a beer and offered one to Josh. "My brother has legal contacts and we may need their help. I'm sorry mate, I know you don't need this shit right now but if this becomes a police matter you guys will need to know what to say."

Josh grimaced, took the beer, and came to a decision. "I'll tell my mates to trust you," he said.

I called Nick and told him what had happened. I explained Rick's situation and Mary's involvement, I told him about the drugs and how I had gathered the information by promising a lawyer. Nick gave me the number of a lawyer and information on how the boys should handle the situation if things went wrong.

I relayed this information to the group and assured them I would be at their side if things got messy, it made me fell slightly better about manipulating the drug confession from Josh. When we had the boys' story settled I asked Josh and his friends for the real story of what had happened.

Josh, Rick and the three friends had been out clubbing in Kuta before returning to the villa about at four in the morning where they continued drinking into the daylight hours. They had a packet of Es on them which were handed around while they sat by the pool.

At about seven o'clock Mary and her nurse friend came down to the pool carrying a bottle of Jack Daniels. They had also spent the night partying. They joined the boys by the pool and everyone proceeded to get drunk and stoned.

At about ten that morning it was decided amongst the boys that they would have a competition to see who could hold their breath the longest while swimming the length of the pool. The pool at the complex is long and deep, and there is no lifeguard on hand although this is not compulsory under Indonesian law as far as I know. The boys had a few tries and then one of the group decided with stoned logic that the competition would be better if they wore a diver's weight belt.

Josh went first, then his friends and then it was Rick's turn. Unfortunately, nobody took much notice when Rick dove into the water. The party sat a few metres away from the pool and could not see the bottom.

Josh told me that he was unsure how long Rick had spent underwater but he suddenly noticed he had not surfaced. Josh screamed to his friends then jumped in the pool and swam down to the bottom where he found Rick unconscious.

Rick was pulled out of the pool dead but, working together, the nurses managed to bring him back to life. Rick would die another four or five times that morning.

Josh didn't stop there, as soon as the nurses began working on Rick he ran to the security box at the villa complex and demanded they call an ambulance. He spent the next two hours running back and forth, about three hundred metres up steep steps, and demanding the security call the ambulance over and over. Josh would wait to hear the phone call then run back to the pool to check on Rick.

When the ambulance arrived Josh saw his friend into the back then got on a motorbike and followed it to the hospital.

Josh was a switched on guy and I believe he would be a great person to have by your side in a crisis. He was twenty-one when this happened and it is no surprise that he was exhausted by the time I met up with him.

Josh's father sent him away because he stole a car, he came half way around the world and saved a life. Josh's father deserves to know the calibre of his son's personality and it is for this reason that I have used his real name. I hope one day Josh shows this story to his father as I'm sure he would be justifiably proud of his son.

Rick was incredibly lucky to have a friend like Josh and to have so many people in his corner; he would later abuse that luck by doing a runner on the hospital and the ambulance bill. Before Rick did the runner he complained that the ambulance took two hours to arrive and one hour to get to the hospital, also that it was ill-equipped to save his life. Had I been armed with the knowledge that Rick would do a runner, I would have liked to ask how it was possible for a hospital to fully equip their ambulances if people did not pay their bills. I have not used Rick's real name in this book although I would have liked to.

Rick came out of the medically induced coma about three hours later, and, despite what everyone expected, he was fine.

I spoke to Rick a week after the incident and he told me that he had taken Mary and her friend out to dinner to thank them for saving his life. Then he told me that he thought Mary was a bitch and he didn't like her. Despite my personal feelings for Mary I could not help but think that Rick was ungrateful.

Josh and I became friends after this event; we would catch up for a beer once in a while if he was in Kuta, we would have a few drinks then go our separate ways. It was during one of these meetings that I grilled Josh about the Es they had taken on the night of the drowning.

I wasn't happy that he would risk his future by scoring drugs in Indonesia, in my eyes the kid had so much going for him that it would have been a waste. I am no angel but the one thing I steer clear of in Indonesia is the drug scene.

Josh told me he had scored his Es in a seedy café. Rick and Josh were taken to a private booth where they made their order, the drugs were brought into the room, money was handed over and they left.

This was incredibly dangerous. There is a lot of money to be made by dobbing in a couple of rich kids looking to score. The current price for a get-out-of-jail-free card, as I understand it, is AUD$10,000 for every year you might spend in custody. You are expected to plead guilty and to keep the arrest out of the press.

Any press involvement and all bets are off. You will do time and the price for a reduction in that time will skyrocket.

The Divide and Conquer Method
(or *How to Take a Villa from a Westerner*)

1. Gain trust
Gain your victim's trust by being their friend, invite them to your home and to a few of your ceremonies. Always claim to be poor but never ask for money in the early stages. After a few months your victim will be sufficiently softened and ready to manipulate. You will know when the time is right when your victim constantly says to friends in your presence: "We are family. He/she has never once asked me for money."

2. Eliminate the competition
Discredit whomever your target is getting advice from by telling your target that every piece of advice they have received is incorrect and back it up with: "I am Indonesian and I know the rules of my country."

3. Exert your power
When you have discredited the competition, instil as much fear as possible in the situation by using the aforementioned advice giver (or property consultant) as a scapegoat. Explain to the target that they got things wrong and there is a high chance they will lose their villa/land/investment/other. Tell them that because you are Balinese/Indonesian you can help but they will have to pay bribes

to the right people and mention, of course, that you know the right people. Let them know that you can facilitate these transactions.

4. False contract

Employ the services of a notary or some other legal person that you are related to or you know. If you don't happen to know such a person a bribe will suffice. Tell the legal representation that they may charge whatever fees they wish and that they will receive a slice of the pie when the final deal goes through. Then have the target place their property in your name so they can avoid further problems.

Note: You may have to sleep with your victim to expedite this strategy but it is a small price to pay for the riches you will receive.

It surprises me how many people fall for this simple ploy and how many are clients of our company. These customers have been done for different amounts and the scams do not always get to stage four, but the initial stages of this scam do a staggering amount of damage to the creditability of a legitimate company trying to protect the best interests of its clients.

Unfortunately, the targeted Westerners have so much trust in their Balinese friend/brother/sister/boyfriend/girlfriend/husband/ wife that they are unwilling to listen to sensible advice. They will even enlist other Westerners to their cause and suddenly the initial lies of the scam artist become a universal truth.

Monkey Tail and the Legend of The Grey Sardine

It was mid-afternoon on a Friday and I was at work when I received the text from Aaron: "Yo Mal, I am in Bali for two weeks. Could use your help, need to catch up. Aaron".

That the text came on a Friday was a good thing. I had a feeling that Aaron would want to immerse himself in the Kuta nightlife and that could mean anything from clawing my way into bed at three thirty in the morning to nursing a massive hangover for the next two weeks.

I arranged to meet Aaron at a small pub on Legian Street later that afternoon; I hoped we could have a beer and catch up then formulate a plan of attack for the evening. When I arrived at the pub I saw that Aaron was sitting with someone I vaguely recognised, I hadn't seen the guy for about ten years and life hadn't been kind.

Gary was in his late thirties but he could have passed for sixty. He wore his thick steel-grey hair mullet-style; he was short, skinny and sat hunched over, his face was weather-beaten and his complexion pale and flaky. He reminded me of Mr Burns from

"The Simpsons".

Gary could have been somebody's grandpa except for his dress sense—he wore an open flannelette shirt over a Bintang singlet, a pair of dirty cheap board shorts and double-plugger thongs. He looked like an Eighties bogan escaped from a retirement village. I walked over and introduced myself.

Aaron and Gary had been in Bali a week and the locals had taken to calling Gary "The Grey Sardine". It suited him so Aaron and I adopted the name. I joined Aaron and The Sardine at their table and ordered a round of beers.

We had a few drinks and relived old times, at some stage during the chat The Grey Sardine disappeared to the toilet.

Aaron used the opportunity to seek my help. He had a quick look to make sure The Sardine was nowhere in earshot, then leaned over the table and gestured me in. "Mal, do you know any hookers that are not real choosy?" I was a little taken aback by the question. "Um, yeah, maybe," I replied. "Why do you ask?"

Aaron looked left and right to make sure The Grey Sardine was nowhere in range. "It's Sardine. No girl will have him, he gets nothing but knock-backs at home and I doubt he has had sex in the last six years."

"Poor bloke," I whispered.

Aaron nodded, "Yeah, poor bloke. He fucking tries so hard too, I have only ever seen him be nice to girls and all they do is take the piss. They get him to buy drinks all night and then go home with somebody else."

I sympathised with Gary, it's hard to meet women in a place like Australia. "You should tell him to clean himself up a bit mate, dress better, maybe get a haircut."

Aaron held a hand up and stopped me. "Listen mate, I don't have much time. I brought Gary here so he could meet a girl, you know, pay for sex. I figure the little bugger deserves that at least, problem is no hooker will have him."

I laughed. I knew that working girls in Bali could be choosy. They could afford to be, they lived and worked in a tourist town and they were constantly surrounded by young fit surfers. I could imagine a guy who looked and dressed like The Grey Sardine might struggle. I leaned in close. "OK mate, I understand," I said, and felt as though I was part of a little conspiracy. "Although I can't say I blame them."

Aaron, The Sardine and I had a few more beers and after a while a plan started to formulate in my mind. I knew a guy, an expat who had lived in Bali a lot longer than me.

I had seen Tom around town a few times and the girls I saw him with were not what I would call attractive—he did in fact have the worst taste in women I had ever encountered. I excused myself from the table, went around the corner, pulled out my phone and dialled Tom's number.

Tom answered instantly. We got along well and we often had a beer and a joke. "Hey mate how's it going, listen I have a bit of a problem I'm hoping you can help me with."

Tom was a Cockney and his accent was thick and hard to understand. "Yo, Malcolm, how can I help?"

I decided to get right to the point, talking to Tom on the phone was difficult at the best of times—worse when surrounded by Bali traffic. "Do you know any ugly hookers, mate?" I ventured.

There was a moment of silence. "Fuck me Mal, what are you up to? Why the fuck would you want the phone numbers of ugly hookers?"

I could understand Tom's confusion. I thought I should explain myself; my question sounded weird even to me. "I have a mate, he's a nice guy but he ain't pretty, he looks like a sardine. Poor bloke keeps getting knocked back by prostitutes, I'm hoping —"

"He looks like a what?" interrupted Tom.

"A sardine, mate. I'm hoping to find him a nice bad girl that will do the right thing. A girl that is less choosy than average."

The phone went silent. I could almost hear Tom digesting what I'd asked and I dreaded the question I thought was coming.

"OK, I understand about your mate looking like a fish, but what made you think of me?"

I didn't want to offend Tom and I had to think fast. "He looks like a sardine not a fish. I don't know, I'm ringing everyone, your number just came up."

Tom laughed, "Fish, sardine, same fucking thing. Where are you?"

"Legian Street, Goes Art Bar," I replied.

Tom thought for a moment. "I know a guy, have done since I first came to Bali, he hangs out on Legian Street not far from you. He's dodgy but he does the right thing. He'll meet you there soon, his names Ketut, you can ask him for whatever you want."

"Cheers Tom," I said, "you've been a big help." I hung up the phone and walked back to join The Sardine and Aaron. When I entered the bar I winked at Aaron, "Sorted."

Aaron gave me a thumbs up and The Grey Sardine looked over at me. "What's sorted?" he asked.

I didn't want to hurt Gary's feelings so I decided to tell a half truth. "Aaron told me you were interested in meeting a girl, I know a guy, who knows a guy." I pulled out my chair and sat down, "I just gave him a call, he's going to come down and hook you up."

The Grey Sardine smiled. "Cheers bro," he said, and again I felt sorry for him.

I'd been back at the bar all of ten minutes when a seedy-looking Indonesian strolled in and introduced himself as Ketut. "Apa kabar. Are you Mal?" he asked, "I'm Ketut, Tom's friend."

I introduced Ketut to Gary and Aaron and ordered him a beer.

When the beer arrived I walked Ketut outside. "I need a prostitute Ketut, she's not for me she's for my friend."

Ketut smiled and I guessed he was already counting his money. "Which friend wants, the old man want?"

I chuckled. "How did you know?"

Ketut laughed and slapped his thigh. "Ketut guessing. I think that old man because he looks like he needs a prostitute. What name him? Gary, yes?"

"Yeah, his name is Gary but the local people call him The Grey Sardine."

Ketut grabbed his belly and doubled over. "Ya, ya is true, your friend he look like sardine. Which girl your friend the sardine wants?"

I did my best to explain to Ketut what I wanted for The

Grey Sardine. "My friend wants woman not beautiful. He wants woman nice and honest but not young girl, maybe older so she not worried about being with grandpa."

"Ya, I know girl. She live same *kampung* with me. I call her, yes?"

I liked Ketut's no-nonsense attitude, he was straight down to business. "She will come here now?" I asked.

Ketut was already pushing numbers on his phone, "Ya, ya, no problem, she come," he said, "Maybe you look after Ketut, when she come, ya?"

I pulled out a hundred thousand and held it up, "When the girl comes I will give this to you." It was exorbitant for making a phone call, and Ketut would also receive a commission, but I wanted the deal to go through.

Ketut looked up at the note, his eyes narrowed and he smiled. "Ok I call girl now, ya, I bring her Goes Art Bar?"

I patted Ketut on the shoulder, "Yes Ketut, bring girl Goes Art. Not beautiful but not too ugly, ya."

Ketut shrugged concentrated on his phone, "Ya, ya, not beautiful, not ugly, girl good for sardine man."

Five minutes later Ketut came and joined us, he placed his empty beer glass in front of me and sat down. "Girl comes fifteen minutes," he said. I ordered him another beer and we settled down to wait.

The girl arrived half an hour later, she wasn't pretty but she was by no means ugly. She wore thick make-up, was a little overweight and was probably pushing forty. It was a match made in heaven as far as I was concerned.

I felt Ketut had done a good job. I slipped him the hundred under the table and Ketut shoved the money into his pocket. I put an arm about Ketut's shoulder and pulled him close. "He will give her three hundred for a short time," I whispered.

Ketut agreed then stood up from the table and greeted the girl as Heni; he walked over and whispered in her ear. I saw Heni nod and the two of them began conversing in Indonesian.

I used the moment to tell The Grey Sardine that I had organised the girl for him and asked if he thought she was OK. The Grey Sardine gave me a goofy smile. "She's beautiful," he whispered, and I could sense his excitement.

Ketut and the girl finished talking and Ketut introduced her to us before inviting her to sit next to The Sardine.

I leant over and took Heni's hand; I introduced myself, then Aaron and The Grey Sardine. Heni shook the boys' hands and took a seat next to The Sardine. The Sardine smiled at Heni, "Would you like a drink?" he asked.

Heni returned his smile. "Lemonade," she replied. The Sardine ordered and the new couple seemed to get along fine.

Ketut came to my side and placed an arm about my shoulder, "She says OK, three hundred," he whispered. I nodded and shook Ketut's hand; he then thanked me for the beer and disappeared.

Aaron and I remained at the table but we gave Heni and The Sardine space to talk. We quickly became involved in our own conversation and what happened next came as a surprise. Heni finished the lemonade then stood up from the table. "I go!" she said, and picked up her handbag.

The Sardine looked astonished. He glanced at me and blushed

and I immediately felt sorry for him. I looked up at Heni. "What's wrong?" I asked.

Heni fiddled with her handbag, she unzipped it and shoved her phone inside. "Nothing wrong," said Heni, and re-zipped her bag.

I stood up from the table. "Is there problem Heni, I think we already make deal?"

Heni threw her bag down on the table then she pointed at The Grey Sardine. "I not want spend time with him," she said in brutal Indonesian fashion.

I couldn't believe it. As far as I could tell The Sardine had been the perfect gentleman. I held up my hand and tried to calm her down. "Heni, it's OK," I said, "my friend will pay and he only wants short time."

Heni turned to me and thankfully she switched to Indonesian. "Yang ini saya tidak mau. Kamu OK, teman kamu OK, tidak ada masalah, tetapi orang tua ini saya tidak mau!" she spat in simple enough Bahasa for me to follow. ("I do not want him. You or your friend are OK but I don't want the old man.")

I was devastated for The Sardine. He'd just been refused by an average-looking hooker in public and I had set the whole humiliating thing up, I felt like a real prick.

I did my best to alleviate the situation. "Heni mau dua ratus ribu lagi?" I said in my pidgin Indonesian. "Mungkin lima ratus ribu? Jam kecil ya, ini bagus price." (You want Rp200,000 more Heni? Maybe Rp500,000? Just short time, it's a good price.) I hoped Gary wouldn't realise that I had offered Heni more money.

Heni listened but she wasn't interested. "No want," she

replied in English. She flicked her hair, picked up her purse, turned on her heels and left the bar.

I looked over at The Grey Sardine. "Sorry, man,"

Gary shrugged and sighed, he looked devastated. "Don't worry about it, Mal," he mumbled, and took a sip of his beer.

I decided to make it up to The Grey Sardine. I stretched out my hand to him and he took it. I looked him in the eyes and said, "You and I are going out tonight and I'm going to find you two girls and I promise you they will be better looking than that pig." This seemed to cheer Gary up somewhat but I was only digging a deeper hole for myself.

That night was a long one. The Grey Sardine seemed to have fun, I on the other hand spent most of the night hunting down and chatting up hookers only to get rejected when I introduced them to him. Aaron did his best to help but only got in the way, he was a little too handsome and any girl he brought over inevitably wanted him.

The night was almost over, the dances had been danced, the crowds had thinned and the working girls had wangled their share of alcoholic drinks from patrons seeking their services. I knew that if I was ever going to get The Grey Sardine a woman, that time was now. Unfortunately, he picked this particular time to deliver a bombshell.

Aaron, The Sardine and I were leaning against the bar in a popular Seminyak club, when Aaron turned to me and asked, "Mal, what are the chances of getting more than one girl?"

"The chances are great, if you're willing to pay," I replied stupidly, and instantly regretted it when I saw The Sardine staring at me.

The Grey Sardine rounded on me and grabbed me by the shoulder. "That's what I want," he said. "I've never been with two girls and you said earlier you would get me two."

"No shit, did I say that?" The Sardine couldn't be serious, I thought. I had to think quickly. "Listen Gary, I'm doing the best I can, all the girls here are working but I can't force them to go with you."

I hoped The Grey Sardine would understand. He didn't. He looked at me with big watery eyes, "But I've never been with two girls at the same time, Mal. If you can get me two girls I will pay for a girl to go with you."

It was a deal clincher. "OK, I will make one more round of the bar and see what I can do."

I grabbed Aaron by the shoulder and told him of my plan to search the bar one more time and he agreed to join me. We were about to begin our quest when fate stepped in and lent a hand. A group of girls entered the bar and stood off to our right. There were five and I could tell by the way they scanned the patrons that they were working. I decided to make my move as fast as possible, it was late but there were still a few hungry packs of guys floating about.

I pulled The Sardine aside, I wanted him out of the way. "I need you to do something for me, I want you to go outside and get a taxi. Then I want you to take the taxi over to the Circle K and buy as many vodka drinks as you think you can afford."

The Grey Sardine nodded affably; I took a good look at him and changed my mind. "Hang on a second." I took out my wallet and passed The Sardine a couple of hundred thousand and asked Aaron to do the same. "Just buy shitloads of alcohol, we are going to need to get these girls very drunk. When you have the taxi fully loaded, come to the front door of the club and send me a message. Aaron and I will bring the girls out."

The Grey Sardine turned his back on me, clutching the stash of notes in his hand as he raced for the club entrance. I watched him go, glad that he wouldn't be around when Aaron and I approached the girls. I took a long drink of my beer, worked up my courage, and motioned Aaron to follow. I wasn't one hundred percent sure how I would make things happen but I did have a card up my sleeve and planned to use it.

During the course of the evening Aaron had mentioned that he and The Sardine were sharing a room in one of Bali's swankier hotels. The hotel was plush and empty and happened to have a massive swimming pool right on the beach. I thought the girls would know of this hotel and planned to name drop at the first opportunity. We walked over, introduced ourselves to the girls and wasted no time ordering a round of vodka shooters. When the drinks were brought to the table we held them up and made some stupid toast, then the whole group downed their drinks in one gulp.

Aaron went to the bar to order the next round so I took the opportunity to drop the hotel name and invite everyone to a party by the pool. The girls looked at each other and there was a lot of head nodding and rushed Indonesian, then the girl I guessed was the designated spokeswoman asked, "Do you want all of us to come?"

Aaron arrived back at the table with two drinks each on a tray and we passed out the shooters. I held up my glass and said, "Yes, we can have a big party." I downed the shooter and Aaron and the girls followed suit.

I took my drink and said to the designated spokeswoman, "We have another friend, he is getting a taxi and some drinks. We can meet him outside if you are ready to go." I wanted the girls up and moving, I didn't want them to question or change their minds, so I swallowed my drink and watched as she did the same.

The spokeswoman put down her glass, turned and had a brief conversation with her friends. She turned back to me, "We will come but we are businesswomen." I knew from experience that the initial stages of the deal were the wrong time to talk price.

"Is OK, I understand," I said. "We will have small party, drink and swim, and then we can talk business." I felt it was better to let the girls relax by the pool with a drink before starting the negotiations.

The Sardine's text came through. I felt the vibration but I didn't bother to take out my phone and answer. I just took the girl by the hand. "Come, we talk in taxi." I was unwilling to take no for an answer.

Aaron followed suit, he placed his arms about the shoulders of two girls and moved them towards the door. I turned to the remaining two girls. "Come on, we go," I said, and pumped my fist in the air. "We have pool party!"

Once outside, I saw The Grey Sardine's taxi and didn't break step. I opened the back door and guided three of the girls onto the back seat. Aaron followed and forced his way in, this left five people crammed into the rear of a small Bali cab. The Sardine must have felt right at home.

I climbed into the front seat and pulled the remaining two girls onto my lap. It was dark in the taxi with so many bodies and I was glad for it, the less the girls saw of The Grey Sardine the better.

The driver started to protest and I couldn't blame him, the small taxi was jam packed. "The Paradiso Hotel!" I said, but we didn't move.

I managed to struggle my head up and look over one of the girl's shoulders and saw a worried look on the driver's face. "Paradiso Hotel, Pak!" I managed, before my face was crunched by a giggling girl's elbow.

The driver looked to where my voice had originated, he found my eyes and shook his head. "Too many people," he said. "If Polisi catch big trouble."

This presented a problem. I didn't want the girls to be split up and didn't want them to get a good look at The Grey Sardine. "I will give you a nice tip," I managed, before a shoulder obscured my view.

I waited for the car to start moving but it didn't budge. "Shit," I swore into the girl's armpit.

I wiggled my face through sweaty skin and again found the driver. "Please, sir," I said. "I'm dying here."

The driver waggled a finger at me. "Polisi," he said, and then he faded from view.

I understood the driver's concern but I also knew it was a lie. It was about two in the morning and the cops in Bali didn't work that late. The girls were heavy on my lap and the car was filled with the smell of cheap perfume, the air was cloying and I felt a little sick. I wanted to move fast so I could get the window down and let in some fresh air.

"Hey guy's it looks like we won't be going anywhere," I screamed, and two bottles of Mix Max were passed to the front. The girls on my lap didn't hesitate; they grabbed a bottle each, opened them and started drinking.

I could hear muffled giggles and laughter coming from the back seat, it seemed I'd been given my answer. I shoved my face into one of the girl's shoulders and she lifted an arm to accommodate my movement, my head now poked through between her arm and her breast. Miraculously I could see the horrified driver's face again. "I will double the fare," I bellowed, "but you have to leave now."

The driver smiled and nodded. "Ya, OK, you make double and we go."

We must have looked a sight to the sleepy security guards at Paradiso Hotel: five scantily clad hookers, two drunken Australians and a reject from a John West factory.

We tumbled out of the taxi into the hotel foyer and the security didn't seem to care. I was happy that the girls hadn't seemed to notice The Grey Sardine and pushed him in front and did my best to distract the girls. We waved our brightly coloured Mix Max bottles at the security and they waved us by. The girls had been promised a pool party, and they definitely wanted a swim, so we made our way up to the boys' hotel room to collect a few towels.

The girls piled into the bathroom, all five of them, and I

figured they went to do their make-up and hair. Why they did this before they went swimming was a mystery but I have never really understood women or what they do.

Surprisingly, The Grey Sardine said he was tired and he wanted to have a sleep and wait for us in the room. Aaron and I tried to talk him out of it as the whole thing had organised for him, but The Sardine refused. He jumped into his bed, ignored us, and fell asleep.

We gave up on The Sardine and gathered up drinks, towels, and girls into our arms and left Gary to his nana nap. We took the back stairs to avoid security and headed down to the hotel pool.

The pool was deserted. It was a beautiful Balinese night and the girls stripped down to their knickers, while Aaron and I jumped in naked.

No sex took place in the swimming pool. Aaron and I took turns at teaching the girls to swim and our little half-naked group of semi-drunks frolicked and laughed together underneath the fat Bali moon. We split into three groups, Aaron choose the two girls he wanted to be with and I spent most of my time with one girl, I liked her and we seemed to get along. The other two girls stuck together and chatted, there was an understanding that they would end up with The Grey Sardine. I have no idea what they thought about this but at least they were drunk and getting drunker. We spent an hour in the hotel pool before the girls began to get cold; it was then decided to head back to the room.

When we arrived back at the room we found The Sardine sound asleep, so Aaron and I threw bottle tops at him, as friends do. The girls piled into the bathroom again, they seemed to love the hot water and fought over the shower. In the end they all piled in together. I would have loved to join the girls, and I'm sure Aaron felt the same, but we were not allowed in.

We tried to wake The Sardine but he wouldn't budge. We tried everything we could think of, we even dribbled iced water on his head, but we received no reaction and eventually decided he was a lost cause. I asked Aaron to help and we lifted The Grey Sardine off his bed as I thought I might need it. We carried him to a small couch and gave him a rug and a pillow—The Grey Sardine seemed content.

This left Aaron and I with a dilemma. We had five girls in the room that would need to be paid, a deal had been struck, and although a price had yet to be set the girls would expect a fee whether they slept with us or not. We could have sent two girls home with less payment but that seemed unfair. Aaron came up with a plan, "Why don't we let all the girls stay?"

The girls had shown us that they had no problems being naked together and Aaron had already spoken to his two girls about sleeping with him. I decided it sounded like a good idea.

This left us with a problem. Aside from cutting one of the girls in half we had to decide who took on the extra girl. After some deliberation, we decided on a simple game of Rock, Scissors and Paper.

As luck would have it I won, so I brushed the skin flakes out of The Sardine's bed, climbed in and waited for the girls.

Aaron forced his way into the bathroom and returned a moment later with two girls. He pulled them into bed and thankfully covered up with a blanket. I hopped from the bed and turned off the light—I didn't want to watch Aaron having sex.

This left me with three. I had no idea what I was going to do with so many bodies but I was willing to give it a try so I opened the bathroom door and asked the girls to join me then climbed back into bed. The girls came in a group, they were all jiggling beasts and giggles. They climbed into bed beside me, around me, and on top of me.

I had never been in bed with three naked bodies before, it was strange but I had little choice but to go with the flow; it was a ding, ding, throw-your-genitals-into-the-ring moment. I kissed each of the girls and tried to spend a few seconds with all, there was a lot of laughter, a lot of breasts and way too many hands.

The girls groped and pinched and wrestled, it was reminiscent of a pile-on during a sleep over—it was more grapple than sex. I felt like I was tangled up with a bunch of squirming puppy dogs, it was fun, and funny, for a moment, and then something went horribly wrong.

I slid my hand down one of the girls and discovered something that shocked me—it felt like a small hard penis. No way, I thought, it couldn't be.

I tried to think if any of the girls had seemed masculine and replayed the night in my mind, I tried to remember the swimming pool, the small glimpses I'd had of the girls in the shower. The girls had all seemed like women, not one of them stood out as being a transvestite, but then what I had touched had felt so much like a small erect penis. I was horrified and more than just a little confused. Had I been mistaken? I had to find out.

Trying not to arouse suspicion I scampered over to the very

left-hand side of the bed and fumbled about with one of the girls. When I cleared her of being a man I lifted her to the side so I could check the next girl. There were only three girls but this proved to be more difficult than it sounds. The room was dark and the girls couldn't keep still. No sooner would a girl end up on my left than she would be climbing back over me to rejoin the action. I would try and hold her back and then one of the girls would climb over me to get to her. The girls would meet in the middle and become entangled on top of me, then they would roll either left or right to meet up with the other girl.

Confused, I would have to start again. It seemed like I fumbled about between legs for an eternity. I finally figured I'd been mistaken and was about to give up when suddenly I hit the jackpot. When I grabbed one of the girls I felt a small hard candle of flesh that to mind could have only been a dick. I pulled my hand away, slid out of bed and ran to the bathroom to think.

I had to work out what to do. There was no way I wanted a man in my bed and I wouldn't be going back if there was, but then there were still two females in the bed and they were beautiful and naked and willing ... how could I give that up? I marched bravely back into the room to confront the man in my bed. I wanted him gone.

The girls tried to drag me back into their wonderful warm pool of laughter and lust but I resisted. I switched on the bedside light and pulled back the blanket, I was determined to expose the imposter and I fully expected to see an erect penis staring back at me. What I saw shocked me even more.

One of the girls was lying on her stomach and protruding

from her back, just above her arse, was a small tail; the appendage was no more than two inches long and it wouldn't have looked out of place on a Doberman. I stared at the tail for a second then threw the blanket back over the girls before anyone else could see. I was stunned, yet relieved. I sat down on the side of the bed and lit up a smoke, I needed time to think. Then I looked over and saw three lumps writhing away underneath the blanket in the other bed it gave me an idea.

I didn't want to embarrass the girl with the tail, she was a lovely creature and had been incredibly fun all night, but the whole tail-feeling-like-a-dick thing had sort of put me off. I wasn't really keen on sharing my bed with her anymore and I wanted to get rid of her without creating a fuss or making her feel uncomfortable. I called out to Aaron and one by one three heads popped out from underneath his blanket, two at the pillow end and another from the other end of the bed.

"How's it going in there, mate?" I asked.

Aaron smiled. "Can't complain," he replied, and the other two heads sniggered.

From the corner of my eye I saw the girl with the tail watching and felt she was worried that I would embarrass her. "Listen mate, I need a favour. Three girls is just too much for me," I said awkwardly. "I don't think I can handle it, if you know what I mean? Any chance you can deal with another, mate?"

Aaron didn't even take the time to think. "Fuck, yeah," he said, and asked the head next to him. "What do you think, love, do we have room for one more?"

The girl sniggered and I figured she had given her approval, then the head from the foot of the bed said, "I want." I looked over at the girl with the tail and without asking she climbed out my bed.

I felt relieved but I also felt like a bit of a wanker. I climbed back into bed with my two girls and tried to put the whole event out of my mind. It wasn't so difficult.

The romp continued until the early hours, punctuated with sighs, groans and laughter. Eventually I climbed out of bed exhausted and the girls cuddled into each other. I went out onto the hotel balcony for a smoke and a short time later Aaron joined me.

"Thanks for that, Mal.

Did you know that girl has a tail?" he asked.

I suddenly felt guilty and I tried to explain myself, "Yeah I did, it sort of put me off. Sorry about that."

Aaron laughed and slapped me on the back, "Are you kidding me, I loved it."

I turned to face him, "You what?"

Aaron beamed and I could tell he was happy, "I said I loved it. The other two got jealous, I just wanted to be with monkey tail."

I laughed despite myself. "Monkey tail, is that what you call her? You can't call her that!"

"Yes I can," he chuckled, "that's what I call her and she likes it. I'm going to get her phone number and I want to see her again."

I let the conversation rest, took a long draw on my smoke and waited for sunrise.

When the sun broke the horizon I decided it was time to leave and I walked back into the room. I was in for one more shock on what had been a very strange night.

The Grey Sardine had somehow pulled himself out of his drunken sleep and climbed into his bed. He was now happily canoodling my two girls.

I have to give it to the guy, he was a trier. As for the girls, they didn't seem to mind. I left the room as fast as possible as I had no desire to witness The Grey Sardine in the throes of passion—some things are just too horrible to behold.

As I walked from the hotel I couldn't help but think how bizarre it was to live in a place like Bali, you just never knew where a night would take you.

Aaron continued to see Monkey Tail and when he returned to Australia he remained in touch. He even sent her small amounts of money to help her get by. He seemed to be falling in love with the girl until one day he misplaced his phone, lost her number and sadly the two of them lost contact.

Aaron asked me to find her again but no matter how hard I tried I never could.

Big Berlin Bouncers
Date Ladyboys

A major cause of fights in Bali is girls or, more specifically, hookers.

What a lot of blokes don't realise, unless they live in Bali, is that although their Balinese girlfriend professes to love them, as soon he gets on the plane home and waves goodbye, the girl wipes away her tears with one hand and sends a text to another guy with the other.

One night, I was in a bar with Billy, his wife and her friend. Billy had spent a long time in Australia and all we wanted was to enjoy a quiet night and share a little gossip amongst old friends. The two girls took a seat and chatted and Billy and I found a quiet corner of the bar so that we could be alone and talk. Billy and I had not been talking long when a pretty girl of about twenty-eight strolled over and started to hover around us.

Leli was a new kid on the block otherwise she would have known that Billy was happily married and that it was more a family get-together than a night out. Leli is now a long-term Bali working girl and I know her quite well—I would even call her a friend.Billy and I were deep in conversation when a young Aussie guy trundled over and stood between us and Leli. He held out his hand and introduced himself as Alan.

Billy and I stopped talking and shook Alan's hand, then politely told Alan that we were brothers and had not seen each other for a long time. We said that we would like to be left alone as we had family business to catch up on, wished Alan a nice holiday in Bali and sent him on his way. Alan disappeared into the crowd and Billy and I went back to our discussion. Leli still lingered but as I said Billy and I found her harmless.

A few moments later a huge German guy turned up holding hands with a ladyboy—after years living in Bali, Billy and I could tell she was a ladyboy right away but the German seemed to have no clue. The German pushed in front of Leli, told us that he was friends with Alan and introduced himself as Hans. He then introduced us to his fiancée. Hans told us that he was taking his fiancée home to meet his parents. We thought this funny, as Hans had no idea that he was dating a man, and Billy and I would later imagine the parents' reaction when they got to meet their new son-in-law, but at the time we weren't so interested in Hans, his holiday or his sex life.

Hans liked to chat and despite Billy and I doing our best to show him we were not interested he told us about his girlfriend/boyfriend, the business he wanted to set up in Bali and the fact he was a weightlifter and doorman back in Berlin.

The last two topics were probably designed to send a message but Billy and I were distracted and it wasn't until later that I would piece this together after what eventually transpired. Billy and I thought little of it and we sent Hans on his way as fast as possible, again we said that we were brothers and we wanted to be left alone.

A few moments later Alan turned up again and tried to force his way into our conversation. Billy looked at me and said, "What are we, the only two people in the bar? Why do these people keep coming up to us?" Once again we explained to Alan that we weren't really interested in a conversation and that although we might seem rude it was because we wanted to catch up and discuss family matters.

We continued talking but were soon interrupted again, this time by Hans's brother, Peter. Peter talked about his holiday, his brother Hans and their friendship with Alan, and how much of a good time they'd all been having as a group. Peter also mentioned that his brother was a well-known doorman in the Berlin nightclub scene. Billy and I sent Peter on his way but over the course of the next few hours the group visited constantly.

Each time we politely told the friends were that we wanted to be left alone but they seemed to get pushier as the night wore on. Eventually we began to suspect that we were being set up and after discussing the intruders we came to the conclusion that Leli was the root of the problem.

Billy and I noticed that every time Alan came over he stared at Leli like a lovesick puppy and for her part Leli did her best to ignore him. Things came to a head when Peter came over for the umpteenth time and pushed between Billy and me. He stood face to face with Billy, stared at him aggressively and asked, "Why are you trying to ignore us?"

"What is it with these people?" asked Billy before pushing

Peter on the shoulder. "Just go away mate, we just want to be left alone."

Peter was a big guy with an immense barrel chest and he tried to use his weight against Billy, he rammed him with his chest and screamed something in German. Billy didn't mess about, he took Peter down with one punch.

Peter fell backwards and the crowd behind the big German went down with him. As he fell back it split the crowd and I saw Alan standing in the corner watching. He had a smile on his face and seemed to enjoy what he had started. I had no doubt that Alan was behind the night's events and that he'd set his German friends against us.

I took off from behind Billy, jumped the fallen crowd and launched myself at Alan. "You fucking started this." I screamed and slammed a shoulder into Alan's chest which flung him against the wall. I grabbed Alan by the hair, pulled his head down and slammed three punches into his face. It was a stupid mistake. Normally Billy and I would fight together and if one fell the other would protect or pull up the fallen person. I was incredibly angry that Alan had caused Billy and me to become involved in what I saw as his petty jealousy over a working girl who we were not interested in. Unfortunately, when I charged Alan I left Billy vulnerable and he suddenly had two big Germans to contend with.

Alan and I fought and I gained the upper hand but this meant I had my back to Billy and I could not see what was going on. The whole pub turned on Billy and me. Evidently, Alan, Hans and Peter were regulars and the Indonesians sided with them.

I do not know what happened to Billy over the next few

minutes; one moment I had Alan against a wall and the next I was surrounded by six Indonesians throwing punches and kicks at my head. I covered up and moved back as punches and kicks flew at me from all directions and suddenly I realised I had somehow ended up outside the bar, about thirty feet from where I had started brawling with Alan.

I was still surrounded by angry Indonesians and they were still taking pot-shots but I had tucked myself into a corner and it offered me some protection. I was no longer taking punches and kicks from behind. I did my best to fend of the Indonesians but then the owner of the bar charged at me from the other side of the street. He jumped in the air and stupidly tried a Bruce Lee-style kick to my face. I managed to catch his foot and shoved him backwards—he landed on his arse. The Indonesians around me went to the owner's rescue and left me alone long enough to spot Billy in trouble in the middle of the road.

Hans, the German bouncer, was on Billy's back and had him in a stranglehold. Billy was surrounded by Indonesians who were taking the opportunity to launch running kicks at his face. He had no way to protect himself and I became furious. I charged past the owner and the Indonesians and ran over to him. I shoved the Indonesians surrounding Billy aside and screamed at Hans to let go of my brother.

Hans turned his face to me and he could see that he was now vulnerable. The Indonesians had backed off and all I needed to do was level a boot at Han's head and he would have been done for. Hans backed down. "I'll let him up," he said "but he has to stop fighting."

"He'll stop, let him up!" I screamed.

Hans released his grip slightly and Billy sucked in a lungful of air. I stepped closer to Hans, "Let him the fuck up!"

Hans finally relented and let Billy loose, he stepped back and I grabbed Billy by his torn shirt and pulled him to his feet.

Hans weaved his way back through the crowd and disappeared and Billy and I were left surrounded by about twenty angry Indonesians. The Indonesian pub bouncer was a huge, muscle-bound, tattooed-up guy who wanted the fight to continue. He stepped forward and his support moved with him.

Billy and I were shoulder-to-shoulder but we stood no chance. Billy was struggling for air and we were heavily outnumbered. We moved back and found ourselves forced against a wall.

The Indonesian bouncer at the head of the group made a move to slap Billy. Billy reacted with a super-human effort and not only dodged the slap but clocked the bouncer on the chin with a left hook that rocked him to the core. The bouncer became wary and moved in slower but he still threw another punch. I tried to protect Billy and stepped in front and took the punch on my chest over my heart. The punch hurt like hell and I suffered the pain of the blow for months to come. The force of the hit shoved me backwards and Billy caught me.

Billy screamed and pushed me aside. I hunched over and tried to get my breath back while Billy launched a combination of blows at the bouncer. The bouncer must have realised he faced a tiger because he backed away from Billy's onslaught and suddenly didn't seem to want things to continue. I managed to pull myself up and Billy and I once again stood shoulder-to-shoulder, we held our ground and faced the bouncer and his pack. The bouncer finally relented. He made a gap in the crowd, pointed down the road and screamed, "You go!"

I put my arm about Billy's shoulder and we walked a small distance then turned and faced the bouncer and his group. We walked backwards down the road and made sure we didn't take our eyes off the crowd. We made it about thirty metres before I noticed Alan push through the crowd and start following us. Alan came close and started to yell at Billy and me, "You fucking cowards. You see what you get when you mess with us!"

Billy and I kept moving but I slowed down to let Alan catch up. Billy knows me very well and he knew what I was doing. "Mal, I'm hurt, mate," he said. "I can't fight anymore."

I was worried about Billy, he had taken a lot of kicks and was severely injured but I was angry that Alan had set us up and that he wanted to boast. "I know mate," I replied. "Do you think you will be able to run if we need to?"

Billy looked at me and smiled, "I'll be okay."

"OK, mate, just keep moving and don't worry about me. I'll be back with you in a second."

Alan finally caught up and came on all swagger and bullshit. He thumped his chest. "You fuckheads see what you get when you make trouble with me!" he screamed.

I was seething. Alan had set Billy and me up over a hooker he'd fallen for and I wanted to kill him. I stopped moving back and I stepped forward. "Yeah, is that what you think, cunt?" I said.

Alan glanced over his shoulder and looked for the protection that was no longer with him. He turned back to me and I saw a glimmer of fear in his eyes. I hit Alan with everything I had and I collected him with a nice hard punch to the jaw. He flew backwards and hit the ground unconscious. I wanted to stomp Alan there and then. I had so much anger in me that given the chance I would have done to him what the Indonesians had done to my little brother. I didn't get the chance.

The Indonesians saw Alan go down and they surged towards Billy and me. I turned and called for Billy to run and that's what we did. I have no idea how far they followed us but we made it safely back to Billy's hotel room. Billy's Indonesian wife and her friend turned up at the hotel a half an hour later and told us the crowd was searching for us on the streets of Kuta. Billy and I stayed in the hotel, we were both hurt but Billy had borne the brunt of the attack.

Despite our injuries Billy and I returned to the bar the following night. We didn't want to court trouble but we did want to show our faces. The bar owner immediately came over and spoke to us. He apologised for the previous evening and offered us free drinks—he even had all his staff, including the bouncer, apologise one by one.

The owner sat at our table and told us that he had discovered who had started the fight and now realised that Billy and I had not been at fault. He said that Alan and the two Germans were now banned from the bar and that if they turned up they would be dealt with.

Eventually Leli and I became friends and she told me that she did in fact sleep with Alan and that he had fallen in love with her, but to her the liaison had been nothing more than a business transaction. She said she'd been hanging around us in the hope that we would scare Alan away as he had been stalking her. She said that she hadn't meant to cause us any harm and I believe her.

I have no doubt that Billy and I were targeted that night because a stupid tourist thought he had found love with an Indonesian prostitute.

Empty Barstool

One of the many reasons a lot of expats and tourists come a cropper in Bali is the lack of enforced drink-driving rules. It's a bit of an anomaly that Indonesia has the largest Muslim population in the world yet a large part of its tourism industry is built on the availability of alcohol. I can imagine it being a bit of a thorn in the side of the more radical Islamic groups in Java, Sumatra and other parts of the country that in Bali the Bintang flows freely.

While riding home drunk one night, I failed to take a corner and slammed into a brick wall doing forty kilometres an hour. I took the wall on my shoulder—years of playing Australian rules football as kid probably helped—but the bike hit the wall, flew in the air and came down on top of me, breaking one of my ribs.

I didn't know what had happened, I have no memory after the initial crash and it wasn't until a bunch of Indonesians lifted the bike of me that I started breathing. They also tried to charge me for the help, stole my wallet, my camera and my dinner, but hey, at least they pulled the motorbike off me. This incident taught me that I was stupid to ride when drunk but one event shocked me to the core and stopped my drink-driving in its tracks.

Phil was a heavy drinker and a rat-bag, but he was always

ready with a smile and he was always respectful to the locals. He also had a great deal of friends and this was revealed by the turnout for his wake and the very real tears they shed at his passing.

Phil and I were drinking at a pub on Legian Street on the night of the accident, we were both drunk but it wasn't long after my first accident and I was wary of driving too drunk. I told Phil that I was going home and I suggested he do the same. Phil decided to stay for one more beer and the next afternoon I received the phone call from Phil's best friend. "Mal, I don't know how to tell you this but Phil is dead. He died in a motorbike accident last night. We're all meeting at the bar if you want to come down." Strangely, I happened to be sitting in the very same pub only in a corner. I was entertaining a group of family and I'd seen a few people I knew at the front bar but had avoided them as I didn't want to mix the groups.

The news fairly rocked me, there was something terrible about the guy I had spent time with the night before dying the next day. I could still remember what we'd talked about, the jokes we had made and the laughter we had shared. I made my excuses to my family and went to join the solemn group at the front bar.

It was an incredibly sad occasion. Five or six blokes sat in silence and nobody was sure what they should say. "He was a good bloke," came up quite regularly and punctuated the silence.

The story of Phil's accident and what had happened took a little time to come out, there were few witnesses but things were eventually pieced together.

Phil stayed for a few more drinks after I left the bar; he apparently switched from beer to Scotch for some reason and stumbled from the bar at about one in the morning. Phil lived close to Nusa Dua, a long way from Kuta and about a thirty-minute ride away from the pub where we'd drank in together. Phil drove on the bypass and because it was late at night and there was little traffic he would have been riding at a good speed. He drove the roundabout on the bypass—close to the big statue that connects Kuta, Sanur, Seminyak and Nusa Dua—and a taxi must have got a call at the same time and pulled out in front of him.

Phil took the taxi on its side. He broke an arm and a leg in the initial collision and the taxi was left with dents in its rear corner and driver's door. Phil ricocheted off the taxi and across the lane, lost control of the motorbike, came off and slammed into the road. Phil would have lived—albeit badly injured—bar one thing: he wore a cheap motorbike helmet and a tiny piece of plastic from the visor broke off and lodged itself in his head. But this wasn't the end of the story.

The taxi driver who collided with Phil picked him up from the road, placed him in the back of his taxi and made his way to the nearest hospital. Phil was still conscious and his faculties were intact enough to make a phone call to his best friend from the taxi.

The friend didn't answer his phone, it was one forty-five in the morning and he had it switched to silent. When the taxi arrived at the international hospital Phil was unconscious. Had he remained conscious, he may have been able to plead his case or make some kind or promissory gesture. The hospital staff asked for cash or some kind of credit card before they would treat Phil but his wallet contained just Rp10,000 and the hospital staff turned him away.

The taxi driver didn't stop there. He made his way to another international hospital and tried to get them to admit Phil. Unfortunately they too turned him away because he lacked cash or credit cards. The driver was left with little choice. He knew Phil needed urgent medical care so he drove Phil to Sanglah Public Hospital in Denpasar, a thirty minute journey. The driver took it slow so he didn't cause Phil further damage.

They arrived at the public hospital at about four in the morning and the staff did all they could to save his life but Phil died at 6 am.

Ever since Phil's death I have travelled around Bali with at least a few cards in my wallet and I always try and hold some cash. I have a Visa card linked to an account that contains only sixty dollars. It doesn't matter, this card could save my life as it shows that I have money available. I would recommend this to any person that wants to ride a motorbike in Bali. I would also like to remind all people that the helmets available are not made to international standards; they are in fact worthless replicas.

This book is dedicated to Phil.